COOK FRESH YEAR-ROUND

SUMMER

FROM

FINE COOKING

from the editors and contributors
of *fine cooking*

The Taunton Press

The Taunton Press
Inspiration for hands-on living®

The Taunton Press, Inc., 63 South Main Street
PO Box 5506, Newtown, CT 06470-5506
e-mail: tp@taunton.com

Copy editor: Nina Rynd Whitnah
Indexer: Heidi Blough
Jacket/Cover design: Stacy Wakefield Forte
Interior design: Stacy Wakefield Forte

Recipes from: Pamela Anderson, Jennifer Armentrout, Jessica Bard, David
Bonom, Scott Conant, Lynne Curry, Ronne Day, Judith Fertig, Dan George,
Fanny Gerson, Dabney Gough, Arlene Jacobs, Sarah Jay, Elizabeth Karmel, Eva
Katz, Alison Ehri Kreitler, Ruth Lively, Ivy Manning, Domenica Marchetti, Denise
Mickelsen, Aimee Olexy, Liz Pearson, Melissa Pellegrino, Caprial Pence, Nicole
Rees, Andrea Reusing, Julissa Roberts, Mark Scarbrough, Samantha Seneviratne,
Maria Helm Sinskey, Joanne Smart, Adeena Sussman, Bill Telepan, Marc Vetri,
Annie Wayte, Joanne Weir, Bruce Weinstein, Shelley Wiseman

The following names/brands appearing in *Summer* are trademarks: Diamond
Crystal®, Morton®, Peychaud's®, Popsicle®, St. Germain®, Sandeman®

Library of Congress Cataloging-in-Publication Data
CookFresh year-round : seasonal recipes from Fine cooking /author, editors of
    Fine cooking.
       pages cm
    Includes index.
    ISBN 978-1-63186-014-0
1. Seasonal cooking. 2. Cookbooks. lcgft I. Taunton's fine cooking. II. Title: Cook
    Fresh year-round.
    TX714.C65428 2015
    641.5'64--dc23
                        2014039388

Printed in China
10 9 8 7 6 5 4 3 2 1

summer

contents

watermelon mule

YIELDS ABOUT 2½ CUPS

¾ cup seeded watermelon chunks
2 fl. oz. (¼ cup) vodka
1 fl. oz. (2 Tbs.) fresh lime juice
1½ fl. oz. (3 Tbs.) ginger beer
1 lime slice, for garnish

Purée the watermelon in a food processor until smooth; strain. You should have 3 fl. oz (6 Tbs.) juice.

Pour the watermelon juice, vodka, and lime juice into a chilled cocktail shaker and fill with ice. Shake for about 10 seconds then pour into a Collins glass filled with ice. Top off with the ginger beer and garnish with the lime slice.

tip

Ginger beer is similar to ginger ale, but has a more pungent, crisp flavor.

watermelon blush

SERVES 1

½ cup watermelon chunks, seeded if necessary
½ fl. oz. (1 Tbs.) St-Germain®
2 dashes Peychaud's® bitters
Prosecco

Purée the watermelon in a food processor until smooth; strain. You should have 2 fl. oz. (¼ cup) juice.

Pour the watermelon juice, St-Germain, and bitters into a Champagne flute. Top off with Prosecco.

tip

Ripe watermelon has a healthy sheen and a creamy yellow spot on the side that rested on the ground. The fruit should be symmetrical, feel heavy for its size, and sound hollow and dull when thumped. Avoid watermelons that are bruised, blemished, or soft in spots.

peach-basil margarita

SERVES 1

3 large fresh basil leaves, plus small
    sprigs for garnish, if you like
1 Tbs. fresh lemon juice
1 fl. oz. (2 Tbs.) peach liqueur

1½ fl. oz. (3 Tbs.) silver tequila
1 slice ripe peach

Put the large basil leaves, lemon juice, and peach liqueur into a cocktail shaker or mixing glass; crush with a muddler or the end of a wooden spoon for about 10 seconds to release the flavor from the basil. Add the tequila and enough ice cubes to fill the shaker three-quarters full, then stir for about 20 seconds.

Strain into a rocks glass over fresh ice, and garnish with the peach slice and basil sprigs, if using.

strawberry mojito

SERVES 4

11 oz. strawberries, hulled (2¾ cups)
⅓ cup fresh lime juice
¼ cup granulated sugar
10 large fresh mint leaves

1 cup white or amber rum
1 cup seltzer
Mint sprigs, lime wedges, or fresh
    strawberries, for garnish

In a medium pitcher, combine the strawberries, lime juice, sugar, and mint leaves and crush with a muddler or wooden spoon until the sugar is dissolved, about 1 minute. Add the rum and stir gently.

Fill four rocks glasses three-quarters full with ice, divide the mojito among them, and top each with about ¼ cup seltzer. Garnish with mint sprigs, lime wedges, or strawberries.

green grape salsa with scallions and mint

YIELDS ABOUT ¾ CUPS

2 cups seedless green grapes,
    quartered
½ medium green bell pepper, cut into
    small dice (about ⅓ cup)
2 medium scallions, trimmed and
    thinly sliced (about ¼ cup)
1 small fresh jalapeño, cored,
    seeded, and minced (about
    1 rounded Tbs.)

3 Tbs. chopped fresh mint
2 Tbs. fresh lime juice;
    more to taste
Kosher salt and freshly ground
    black pepper

In a medium bowl, mix the grapes, bell pepper, scallions, jalapeño, mint, lime juice, and ¼ teaspoon each salt and pepper. Let stand for 10 minutes. Before serving, adjust the lime juice, salt, and pepper to taste.

tip

Serve this salsa alongside spice-rubbed grilled chicken, pork, or turkey. The cool grapes and scallions offset the heat nicely.

grilled eggplant rolls with feta and olives

SERVES 6

1 large eggplant, trimmed and sliced into six ½-inch-thick lengthwise slices
Extra-virgin olive oil, for brushing
Kosher salt and freshly ground black pepper
½ cup crumbled feta

2 Tbs. chopped pitted Kalamata olives
2 Tbs. chopped mixed fresh herbs (such as chives, parsley, and basil); more for garnish

Prepare a medium-hot (425° to 450°F) gas or charcoal grill fire. Brush the eggplant slices with oil and season with salt and pepper.

Grill the eggplant until grill marks form on one side, about 3 minutes. Flip the slices and continue to grill until the eggplant is tender, about 2 minutes more.

In a small bowl, combine the feta, olives, and herbs.

Spread the eggplant slices on a work surface. Put 1 heaping Tbs. of the feta mixture at the wider end of each slice and then tightly roll up. Arrange the rolls seam side down on a platter and finish with a little oil, pepper, and more chopped herbs.

grilled okra with smoked paprika-shallot dip

SERVES 6

1 lb. small okra pods (no longer than 2 inches)
1½ Tbs. canola oil
Kosher salt and freshly ground black pepper
½ cup sour cream
¼ cup mayonnaise
1 medium shallot, grated on the large holes of a box grater (about 2 Tbs.)

1 Tbs. fresh lemon juice
1 Tbs. finely chopped fresh cilantro (optional)
1 tsp. smoked paprika
¼ to ½ tsp. crushed red pepper flakes

Prepare a high gas or charcoal grill fire.

Partially split each okra pod lengthwise, leaving about ½ inch uncut at the stem end. In a large bowl, toss the okra with the oil, 1 tsp. salt, and ¼ tsp. pepper.

In a small bowl, combine the sour cream, mayonnaise, shallots, lemon juice, cilantro (if using), smoked paprika, red pepper flakes, and ½ tsp. salt; set aside.

Grill the okra, flipping once, until the pods are slightly charred and have just split open, about 5 minutes. Transfer to a large platter (don't overcrowd the platter as residual heat and steam can soften the pods). Serve the okra hot with the dip on the side.

smoked trout salad with creamy cucumbers, scallions & dill

SERVES 8

1 medium English cucumber, peeled, halved lengthwise, seed core removed, and thinly sliced (2 cups)
½ cup crème fraîche
¼ cup fresh lemon juice
2 Tbs. chopped fresh dill, plus sprigs for garnish

Kosher salt and freshly ground black pepper
6 Tbs. extra-virgin olive oil
1 lb. smoked trout, skin removed
4 medium scallions, thinly sliced
Eight ¼-inch-thick slices sourdough toast, for serving

In a medium bowl, mix the cucumber with the crème fraîche and 2 Tbs. of the lemon juice. Add the dill and season to taste with salt.

In a large bowl, whisk the remaining 2 Tbs. lemon juice with the olive oil and a pinch of salt. In the bowl, flake the trout into chunks, making sure to remove any bones. Add the scallions and gently toss to combine. Season to taste with salt and pepper.

Make a bed of the cucumbers on a large platter (or divide them among eight small plates); top with the trout mixture. Garnish with dill sprigs and serve with the toast.

grilled eggplant salad with feta, pine nuts & garlicky yogurt dressing

SERVES 4 AS A LIGHT DINNER

2 hearts of romaine, leaves separated (save the small leaves for another use), washed, and dried

1 large eggplant (about 1¼ pounds), cut crosswise into ½-inch slices

5 Tbs. extra-virgin olive oil

Kosher salt and freshly ground black pepper

¾ cup plain yogurt

2 Tbs. fresh lemon juice

1 small clove garlic, mashed to a paste or crushed through a garlic press

¼ tsp. ground cumin

½ cup tightly packed fresh flat-leaf parsley leaves, finely chopped

¼ lb. feta, crumbled (¾ cup)

⅓ cup toasted pine nuts

Put the romaine in a large bowl, cover with a damp paper towel, and refrigerate.

Heat a gas grill to medium high. Brush the eggplant slices with 3 Tbs. of the oil and season with salt and pepper. In a small bowl, combine the remaining 2 Tbs. olive oil with the yogurt, lemon juice, garlic, cumin, and parsley. Season to taste with salt and pepper.

Grill the eggplant slices until softened and browned on the first side, 3 to 4 minutes. Flip them and continue to cook until the eggplant is browned and cooked through, another 3 to 4 minutes. Transfer to a plate.

Portion the romaine onto four plates, lay the eggplant slices on top, and drizzle them with the dressing. Top with the feta and pine nuts.

tip

✦ This salad can be served warm or at room temperature and works well arranged on a platter and served on a buffet table.

spelt salad with cherry tomatoes and zucchini

SERVES 8 TO 10

3 cups spelt
Kosher salt and freshly ground black pepper
½ cup plus 1 Tbs. extra-virgin olive oil; more as needed
⅓ cup red-wine vinegar; more as needed
1¼ cups halved cherry tomatoes
1¼ cups diced zucchini (½-inch dice)
½ cup thinly sliced scallions
3 Tbs. chopped fresh basil
1 Tbs. chopped fresh oregano

Fill a large bowl with cold water, add the spelt, and let soak for 10 to 18 hours. Drain. Bring 7 cups of water to a boil in a 4-quart pot over high heat. Add ¾ tsp. salt. Add the spelt, reduce the heat to a simmer, and cook uncovered, stirring occasionally and adding more boiling water as necessary to keep the spelt covered, until tender, 45 to 60 minutes. Drain and rinse the spelt with cold water to stop the cooking.

Transfer the spelt to a foil-lined rimmed baking sheet, drizzle with 1 Tbs. of the oil, and

tip

Spelt has a chewy texture and nutty flavor, making it a versatile partner in salads. This whole grain needs to be soaked before cooking.

toss lightly to coat. Spread the spelt on the baking sheet and cool completely at room temperature or in the refrigerator.

Put the vinegar in a small bowl and gradually whisk in the remaining ½ cup of oil. Taste and season with salt, pepper, and additional vinegar or oil as needed.

Put the cooked and cooled spelt in a large serving bowl and toss to break up any clumps. Add the cherry tomatoes, zucchini, scallions, basil, oregano, and ½ cup vinaigrette and toss. Taste and season as needed with more vinaigrette, salt, and pepper.

mixed greens with nectarines, gorgonzola & champagne vinaigrette

SERVES 4 TO 6

2 firm-ripe medium nectarines, pitted and thinly sliced
1 tsp. chopped fresh thyme
½ tsp. finely grated orange zest
½ tsp. granulated sugar
Kosher salt and freshly ground black pepper

4 Tbs. extra-virgin olive oil
1½ Tbs. Champagne vinegar
1 tsp. honey mustard
5 oz. (5 cups) mixed baby greens
3 oz. crumbled Gorgonzola

In a medium bowl, toss together the nectarines, thyme, orange zest, sugar, and ½ tsp. salt. Add 1 Tbs. of the oil and toss to coat. Let stand for 10 minutes.

In a small bowl, combine the vinegar, honey mustard, ½ tsp. salt, and a few grinds of pepper. Gradually whisk in the remaining 3 Tbs. of oil.

In a large bowl, toss the greens with enough vinaigrette to lightly coat. Add the nectarines and toss to combine. Divide the mixture among the serving plates, sprinkle with the Gorgonzola, and serve.

grilled radicchio and romaine salad

SERVES 4

1 medium head romaine lettuce
  (about 1 lb.)
1 medium head radicchio
  (about 8 oz.)
½ cup extra-virgin olive oil
1 medium clove garlic
1 small anchovy fillet, rinsed and
  patted dry

2½ Tbs. balsamic vinegar
½ tsp. Dijon mustard
Kosher salt and freshly ground
  black pepper
1½ oz. Parmigiano-Reggiano,
  grated on the large holes of a box
  grater (½ cup lightly packed)

Prepare a medium-high gas or charcoal grill fire, or heat a grill pan over medium-high heat until hot.

Cut the romaine and radicchio in half through the root ends. Rinse the leaves and dry well.

Pour the oil into a large baking dish. Dip the lettuces cut side down in the oil, swirling to coat well; then place them cut side down on the grill. Grill, covered, without turning, until charred and wilted in spots, about 4 minutes. Transfer to a cutting board. Remove the cores and chop the lettuce into bite-size pieces.

Press the garlic and the anchovy through a garlic press into a large salad bowl (or mince by hand). Whisk in the vinegar, mustard, and ½ tsp. each salt and pepper. Transfer the lettuces and any juice from the cutting board to the salad bowl. Add the cheese and toss well.

tomato, chickpea & feta salad

SERVES 6

3 oz. feta, crumbled (about ½ cup)

2 tsp. za'atar

Pinch crushed red pepper flakes

3 Tbs. extra-virgin olive oil

1 lb. cherry, grape, or pear tomatoes, halved

One 15-oz. can chickpeas, rinsed and patted dry

Kosher salt and freshly ground black pepper

1 Tbs. white-wine vinegar

In a small bowl, mix together the feta, za'atar, and crushed red pepper flakes. Add 1 Tbs. of the oil and let sit while you prepare the rest of the salad.

Put the tomatoes in a large bowl. Stir in the chickpeas and season with ¼ tsp. salt and a few grinds of black pepper.

Add the remaining 2 Tbs. oil and the vinegar. Stir in the feta, season to taste with salt and pepper, and serve.

tip

Za'atar is a Middle Eastern spice blend treasured for its savory thyme-oregano flavor.

cucumber, basil & peanut salad

SERVES 6

3 Tbs. seasoned rice vinegar
1 tsp. Asian sesame oil
1 tsp. fresh lime juice
1 tsp. fish sauce
1½ lb. cucumbers

¼ cup torn basil (preferably Thai basil)
¼ cup coarsely chopped salted peanuts

In a large serving bowl, whisk the rice vinegar, sesame oil, lime juice, and fish sauce.

Peel the cucumbers and slice in half lengthwise. Scoop out the seeds and slice diagonally into ¼-inch-thick crescents. Add the cucumbers, basil, and chopped peanuts to the vinaigrette, toss, and serve.

tip

Peel the cucumbers (regardless of variety) so they absorb more flavor. Thai basil provides a slightly sweet, peppery note and a hint of anise, but you can also use Italian basil or mint.

potato salad with garlic scapes, snap peas & scallions

SERVES 6 TO 8

3 lb. small to medium yellow potatoes, such as Yukon Gold, scrubbed
Kosher salt and freshly ground black pepper
¼ lb. garlic scapes, pods and tips removed
6½ oz. sugar snap peas, trimmed and cut on the diagonal into ½-inch pieces (1½ cups)
½ cup mayonnaise
¼ cup extra-virgin olive oil
1 large lemon, finely grated to yield 2 tsp. zest, squeezed to yield 2 Tbs. juice
2 Tbs. plain rice vinegar
½ cup thinly sliced scallions
⅓ cup chopped fresh flat-leaf parsley
⅓ cup chopped fresh mint

Put the potatoes in a 6-quart pot; add 2 Tbs. salt and enough water to cover by 1 inch. Put the scapes on the potatoes. Bring to a boil over high heat, then lower the heat to medium and simmer vigorously until the scapes are just tender, about 5 minutes after the water boils. With tongs, transfer the scapes to a cutting board and cut into ½-inch pieces.

Continue to simmer the potatoes until just tender when pierced with a fork, about 15 minutes

tip

A garlic scape is the flower stem of the garlic plant. Although the entire scape is edible, the pod and tip above it can be fibrous and are best discarded.

more. Add the peas and simmer until crisp-tender, 1 to 2 minutes. Drain the potatoes and peas in a colander. With tongs, transfer the potatoes to a cutting board. Rinse the peas under cold water to stop the cooking and let drain.

While the potatoes cool, whisk the mayonnaise, oil, lemon zest and juice, and ½ tsp. each salt and pepper in a small bowl. In a large bowl, mix the vinegar with 2 tsp. salt and stir to dissolve.

When the potatoes are just cool enough to handle, scrape their skins off with a paring knife and cut them into ¾- to 1-inch pieces. Toss them in the vinegar-salt mixture, and then stir in about half of the dressing. Add the scapes, peas, scallions, herbs, the remaining dressing, and salt and pepper to taste and mix well. Let cool to room temperature before serving.

grilled mushroom, arugula & comté salad

SERVES 4

1 lb. large whole fresh shiitake or
portabella mushrooms, or a mix

5 Tbs. extra-virgin olive oil; more for
drizzling

Kosher salt and freshly ground white
or black pepper

4 cups baby arugula, washed and
dried

¼ cup hazelnuts, toasted and
roughly chopped

2 oz. Comté or Gruyère, thinly sliced
with a vegetable peeler

Fleur de sel or flaky sea salt

Heat a gas grill to medium high or prepare a medium-hot charcoal fire. (Be sure the grate is hot, too.) Wipe the mushrooms clean and trim off the stems. If using portabellas, scrape out the black gills with the side of a spoon. Put the clean whole mushrooms in a large bowl, drizzle with 5 Tbs. of the oil, and gently toss. Sprinkle in a pinch of kosher salt and toss again. Grill the mushrooms directly over the heat until tender and well marked, 3 to 5 minutes on each side. If using portabellas, quickly cut the grilled mushrooms into 1-inch slices.

Portion the arugula among four plates and top with the hot mushrooms. Garnish with the nuts and cheese and a generous drizzle of olive oil. Sprinkle lightly with fleur de sel or other sea salt and a grind of white or black pepper. Serve immediately.

corn and cherry tomato salad with lemon-tarragon vinaigrette

SERVES 4

3 Tbs. extra-virgin olive oil
2 cups fresh corn kernels (from 3 to 4 medium ears)
1 pint cherry tomatoes, halved or quartered (depending on size)

1½ Tbs. fresh lemon juice
1 Tbs. chopped fresh tarragon
Kosher salt and freshly ground black pepper

Heat 1 Tbs. of the oil in a 12-inch nonstick skillet over medium-high heat until shimmering. Add the corn and cook, stirring often, until softened, about 2 minutes. Transfer to a medium bowl to cool slightly.

Add the cherry tomatoes, lemon juice, tarragon, the remaining 2 Tbs. of oil, ¼ tsp. salt, and a few grinds of pepper. Toss and serve.

zucchini and yellow squash ribbons with daikon, oregano & basil

SERVES 8

3 small zucchini (about 1 lb.)

3 small yellow summer squash (about 1 lb.)

1 large daikon radish (about ½ lb.)

20 medium basil leaves, very thinly sliced

2 tsp. chopped fresh oregano

6 Tbs. extra-virgin olive oil

2 Tbs. fresh lemon juice

1 tsp. finely grated lemon zest

Kosher salt and freshly ground black pepper

Small basil leaves for garnish (optional)

Trim the ends of the zucchini and yellow summer squash. With a vegetable peeler, shave the zucchini lengthwise into long, wide strips about 1/16 inch thick. When you get to the center of the zucchini, where the seeds are, turn it over and slice from the other side until you get to the center again. Discard the center. Put the zucchini ribbons in a large bowl. Shave the yellow squash using the same technique and add to the zucchini. Peel off and discard the rough exterior peel of the daikon and then shave the daikon as you did the squash. Add the strips to the bowl with the squash, along with the basil and oregano.

In a small bowl, whisk the olive oil, lemon juice, and lemon zest. Season to taste with salt and pepper. Toss the vegetables with enough of the vinaigrette to lightly coat them (you may not need all of the vinaigrette) and season to taste with salt and pepper. Serve immediately, garnished with the small basil leaves (if using).

tip

Daikon is a large, crisp, juicy Asian radish. It's readily available in Asian markets, but many large supermarkets carry daikon as well.

tomato and fresh green bean salad with crisp prosciutto

SERVES 6 TO 8

6 medium-size ripe red tomatoes, each cut into 6 wedges

Kosher salt and freshly ground black pepper

4 thin slices prosciutto (about 2 oz.)

12 oz. fresh green beans, trimmed and cut into 2-inch pieces

3 Tbs. chopped fresh summer savory, plus fresh sprigs for garnish

2 cloves garlic, minced

2 Tbs. sherry vinegar

¼ cup extra-virgin olive oil

1½ cups yellow and orange cherry tomatoes (or other bite-size tomatoes), halved

Position a rack in the center of the oven and heat the oven to 400°F. Put a large pot of salted water on to boil.

Put the tomato wedges in a colander set over a bowl. Sprinkle with 1 Tbs. salt, toss, and let stand for 30 minutes.

Slice the prosciutto crosswise into ½-inch strips. Arrange on a baking sheet in a single layer and bake until crisp and light golden, about 10 minutes. Set aside.

tip

✖ Summer savory has a peppery flavor and pungent aroma. If you can't find it, substitute fresh thyme or marjoram.

Meanwhile, when the water comes to a boil, add the beans and cook until tender, 4 to 6 minutes. Drain and let cool.

In a small bowl, whisk together the chopped savory, garlic, and vinegar. Whisk in the olive oil to blend. Season to taste with salt and pepper.

Combine the tomato wedges, cherry tomatoes, and green beans in a bowl. Add the vinaigrette, toss, and season with salt and pepper to taste. Transfer to a shallow serving bowl or platter, sprinkle with the prosciutto, and garnish with the savory sprigs. Serve immediately.

spicy corn chowder

SERVES 4

½ lb. thick-cut applewood-smoked
    bacon (6 slices), cut crosswise
    into ½-inch pieces
1 medium yellow onion, cut into
    ½-inch dice
3 scallions, thinly sliced
2 celery ribs, cut into ½-inch dice
1 red bell pepper, stemmed, seeded,
    and cut into ½-inch dice
1 tsp. fresh thyme

5 cups fresh corn kernels
    (from 10 medium cobs)
½ tsp. pure chipotle chile powder
2 cups half-and-half
2 cups lower-salt chicken broth
1 large russet potato, peeled and
    coarsely grated
Kosher salt
Grated white Cheddar, for garnish
    (optional)

Cook the bacon in a 5- to 6-quart Dutch oven
or other heavy-duty pot over medium-high heat
until browned and crisp, about 5 minutes. With
a slotted spoon, transfer the bacon to a paper-
towel-lined plate. Pour off and discard all but
2 Tbs. of the bacon fat.

    Return the Dutch oven to medium-high
heat and add the onion, half of the scallions, the
celery, bell pepper, and thyme. Cook, stirring
occasionally, until the vegetables begin to soften,
about 5 minutes. Add the corn and cook until
softened, about 2 minutes. Stir in the chipotle
powder and cook for 30 seconds.

tip

✦ Don't
substitute
frozen corn here;
the flavor of this
quick chowder
depends on freshly
cut kernels.

Add the half-and-half and chicken broth and bring to a boil. Add the grated potato, lower the heat to medium, and cook, covered, until the potato is cooked through, about 10 minutes. Season to taste with salt and transfer to four large soup bowls. Garnish with the reserved bacon and scallions, and the cheese, if using, and serve.

gazpacho

SERVES 4 OR 5

1¾ lb. ripe tomatoes, cored and
    coarsely chopped (about 4 cups)
½ medium green bell pepper,
    stemmed, seeded, and coarsely
    chopped (¾ cup)
½ small red bell pepper, stemmed,
    seeded, and coarsely chopped
    (½ cup)

¼ cup packed torn fresh bread,
    such as a soft baguette or slice
    of white sandwich bread, plus
    ¼ cup packed ½-inch cubes
    (crusts removed) for croutons
9 Tbs. good-quality extra-virgin
    olive oil; more for drizzling
2 tsp. sherry vinegar
1 small clove garlic
Kosher salt
Ground cumin
1 Tbs. chopped fresh cilantro

Put the tomatoes, bell peppers, torn bread, 6 Tbs. of the olive oil, the
vinegar, garlic, 1 tsp. salt, and a pinch or two of cumin in a blender. Pulse
until coarsely puréed, then blend until very smooth, 4 to 5 minutes
(it may be a bit frothy). Season to taste with salt and refrigerate until
very cold, at least 1 hour and up to 2 days.

Heat the remaining 3 Tbs. olive oil in an 8-inch skillet over medium
heat. Add a bread cube; if it sizzles immediately, add the remaining
cubes (if it doesn't, continue to heat the oil). Cook, stirring, until golden-
brown, about 1 minute. Transfer to paper towels to drain and cool.

Taste the gazpacho before serving; adjust the seasonings as
needed. Serve drizzled with oil and garnished with croutons and cilantro.

minestrone with green beans and fennel

SERVES 4 TO 6

3 Tbs. extra-virgin olive oil
2 medium cloves garlic, smashed
½ lb. green beans, trimmed and cut into 1-inch pieces
1 small fennel bulb, quartered, cored, and cut into ¼-inch dice
Kosher salt and freshly ground black pepper
1 quart lower-salt chicken broth
One 14½-oz. can diced tomatoes

One 15½-oz. can cannellini beans, rinsed and drained
½ cup dried ditalini pasta or small elbows
½ cup freshly grated Parmigiano-Reggiano; more for sprinkling
6 large fresh basil leaves, coarsely chopped

Heat the oil and garlic in a medium saucepan over medium heat until the garlic begins to brown, 2 to 3 minutes; discard the garlic. Raise the heat to medium high, add the green beans, fennel, and ¾ tsp. salt, and cook, stirring, until the beans and fennel begin to soften and brown in places, 5 to 7 minutes. Add the broth and the tomatoes with their juices and bring to a boil. Add the cannellini beans and pasta and return to a boil. Reduce the heat to a simmer, cover, and cook until the pasta and green beans are completely tender, 10 to 12 minutes.

Stir in the cheese and basil and season to taste with salt and pepper. Serve sprinkled with additional cheese.

roasted carrot soup

SERVES 4

1 lb. carrots, peeled and cut into 3-inch lengths
1 Tbs. olive oil
1 Tbs. unsalted butter
½ medium onion, cut into medium dice (to yield about ¾ cup)
1 large rib celery, cut into medium dice (to yield about ½ cup)
1 Tbs. minced fresh ginger (from about ½-inch piece, peeled)
2 cups homemade or lower-salt chicken broth
1 tsp. kosher salt
⅛ tsp. ground white pepper
Chopped fresh chives or chervil for garnish (optional)

Position a rack in the center of the oven and heat the oven to 375°F.

Put the carrots in a medium baking dish (in a single layer without touching) and drizzle them with the olive oil. Toss them to coat well and roast, stirring once halfway through roasting, until they're tender, blistered, and lightly browned in a few places, about 1 hour.

Melt the butter in a medium (at least 3-quart) heavy saucepan set over medium heat. Add the onion and cook until it's translucent and fragrant, 2 to 3 minutes. Stir in the celery and ginger and cook until the celery softens a bit and the onion starts to brown, 4 to 5 minutes. Add the roasted

tip

The ginger provides a nice, throat-warming heat to this soup, which tastes best if it sits in the fridge for several hours or overnight.

carrots, chicken broth, salt, pepper, and 2 cups of water. Bring to a boil, reduce the heat to medium low, and cover. Cook at a lively simmer until the carrots are very tender, about 45 minutes. Turn off the heat and let the liquid cool somewhat (or completely).

Purée the soup in a blender in batches, never filling the blender more than a third full, and bearing down firmly on the towel-covered lid so the soup doesn't come flying out. If serving immediately, return the soup to the pot and reheat; garnish with the chives or chervil if you like. Otherwise, refrigerate for up to 5 days; reheat gently and taste for salt before serving.

chilled oven-roasted yellow pepper soup

SERVES 6

8 yellow bell peppers
⅓ cup extra-virgin olive oil; more
   for drizzling
1 large yellow onion, coarsely
   chopped
1 jalapeño, stemmed and seeded
1 Tbs. chopped fresh rosemary

2 cups lower-salt chicken broth
Generous pinch of granulated sugar
Kosher salt or fine sea salt and
   freshly ground black pepper
¼ cup sliced fresh chives
   (¼ inch long)

Position a rack in the center of the oven and heat the oven to 400°F. Put the bell peppers on a rimmed baking sheet and roast in the oven, turning every 15 minutes, until browned and wrinkled all over, 45 to 60 minutes. Remove the peppers from the oven, cover with a dishtowel, and set aside to cool. Seed, peel, and cut the peppers into quarters.

Heat the oil in a 4-quart saucepan over medium heat. Add the onion, jalapeño, and rosemary and cook, stirring occasionally, until the onion starts to brown, 8 to 10 minutes. Stir in the peppers and any accumulated juices, broth, sugar, 1½ tsp. salt, ¼ tsp. black pepper, and

tip

✖ Freeze roasted peppers, along with their juices, in zip-top freezer bags for several weeks. The flesh will be slightly less firm when defrosted. This will be fine if you're using the peppers for sauces, soups, or purées.

1½ cups water. Bring to a simmer over medium-high heat, cover, reduce the heat to low, and simmer for 5 minutes to blend the flavors. Remove from the heat and let cool slightly.

Purée the soup in batches in a blender or food processor. Strain the purée through a fine-mesh sieve into a bowl, using a ladle to push as many of the solids through as possible. Discard the solids in the sieve and refrigerate the soup for at least 3 hours or overnight.

Once chilled, season the soup to taste with salt and pepper. Serve in chilled bowls, sprinkled with the chives. Finish each serving with a drizzle of olive oil.

no-cook tomato sauce

YIELDS 4 CUPS

Kosher salt

1 pound dried pasta

1¼ cups tightly packed fresh flat-leaf parsley leaves

1 medium clove garlic, smashed

1 small hot red chile (like Fresno, serrano, or jalapeño), seeded

2½ lb. ripe plum tomatoes, cut into ½-inch dice

2 Tbs. extra-virgin olive oil

Bring a large pot of well-salted water to a boil over high heat. Put the pasta in the water and cook according to the package directions. Drain and keep warm.

Put the parsley leaves, smashed garlic, and seeded hot chile on a cutting board and mince the ingredients together; transfer to a medium bowl.

Add the tomatoes and olive oil to the bowl with the parsley mixture. Season to taste with salt and serve with the pasta.

spicy shrimp with ginger-garlic long beans

SERVES 4

1 lb. jumbo (16 to 20 per lb.) shrimp, peeled and deveined
¼ cup mirin (sweetened rice wine)
2 Tbs. soy sauce
1 large scallion, thinly sliced (white and green parts)
¼ tsp. crushed red pepper flakes
2 Tbs. untoasted Asian sesame oil
2 tsp. minced garlic
2 tsp. minced fresh ginger
½ lb. Chinese long beans, trimmed and cut into 4-inch lengths

In a nonreactive medium bowl, combine the shrimp, mirin, soy sauce, scallion, and red pepper flakes. Marinate in the refrigerator for at least 1 hour and up to 6 hours.

Heat a 12-inch skillet over medium-high heat. Add the sesame oil, then the garlic and ginger; cook, stirring, until the garlic begins to color, about 10 seconds. Add the beans and stir to coat with the garlic and ginger. Continue to cook, stirring, until the beans start to turn bright green, 1 to 2 minutes.

Add the shrimp and the marinade (be careful of hot steam). Cook, stirring constantly, until the juices have reduced and thickened slightly and the shrimp are pink and curled, 3 to 4 minutes. Serve immediately.

tip

Long beans, the immature pods of a variety of cowpea, are similar in flavor to string beans but are softer and starchier.

fusilli with green beans, pancetta & parmigiano

SERVES 2 TO 3

Kosher salt and freshly ground black pepper
½ lb. fusilli or other twisted pasta
4 oz. pancetta, sliced ¼ inch thick and cut into ½-inch squares (¾ cup)
1 large clove garlic, smashed and peeled
½ lb. green beans, trimmed and cut into 1-inch lengths (2 cups)
2 Tbs. unsalted butter, at room temperature
2 oz. finely grated Parmigiano-Reggiano (1 cup)

Bring a medium pot of well-salted water to a boil. Cook the pasta until just barely al dente, about 1 minute less than package timing. Reserve 1 cup of the cooking water, and drain the pasta.

While the pasta cooks, put the pancetta in a cold 10-inch skillet and set over medium-high heat. When the pancetta starts sizzling, add the garlic and cook, stirring constantly, until starting to brown, 1 minute. Reduce the heat to medium and continue to cook the pancetta until golden but still chewy at the center (taste a piece if you're not sure), an additional 2 to 3 minutes. If the

tip

Beans relinquish sweetness the longer they're stored, so try to use them right away.

pancetta has rendered a lot of its fat, spoon off all but 1 Tbs. of the fat from the pan.

Add the beans to the pan and cook, stirring constantly, until they're crisp-tender, 3 to 4 minutes. Remove the garlic and season the beans with salt and pepper. With the pan still over medium heat, add the pasta, ½ cup of the pasta water, and the butter. Toss to combine. Add another ¼ cup pasta water and ¾ cup of the Parmigiano. Stir well and season to taste with salt and pepper. If necessary, add a little more pasta water to loosen the sauce.

Transfer the pasta to a serving bowl. Grind black pepper over the top and sprinkle with the remaining cheese.

sourdough panzanella with grilled chicken

SERVES 4

½ cup olive oil; more for the grill
Four ¾-inch-thick slices sourdough bread
1 tsp. finely chopped fresh oregano
½ tsp. smoked sweet paprika
Kosher salt and freshly ground black pepper
1 lb. boneless, skinless chicken breast halves, trimmed
3 Tbs. red-wine vinegar
1 anchovy fillet, rinsed
1 small clove garlic
4 medium tomatoes, cut into ¾-inch pieces (3 cups)
1 medium cucumber, peeled, halved lengthwise, seeded, and cut into ¾-inch pieces (1½ cups)
½ small red onion, chopped (½ cup)
¼ cup chopped fresh mixed herbs, such as basil, parsley, cilantro, or mint

Prepare a medium-hot charcoal fire or heat a gas grill to medium high. Clean and oil the grill grate.

Brush the bread on both sides with 2 Tbs. of the olive oil. Grill the bread until well marked, about 1 minute per side. Transfer to a cutting board, cut into ¾-inch cubes, and set aside.

In a small bowl, mix the oregano, smoked paprika, ½ tsp. salt, and ½ tsp. pepper. Sprinkle evenly over the chicken breasts. Grill, turning once, until an instant-read thermometer inserted

tip

For balanced texture, be sure to slice the tomatoes, cucumbers, chicken, and bread about the same size.

into the thickest part of each breast registers 165°F, 10 to 12 minutes total. Transfer to a cutting board, let rest for 5 minutes, and then cut into ¾-inch cubes.

In a large bowl, whisk the remaining 6 Tbs. olive oil and the vinegar. Press the anchovy fillet and garlic clove through a garlic press into the bowl (or mince by hand). Add the bread, chicken, tomatoes, cucumber, red onion, and herbs, and toss well. Season to taste with salt and pepper and serve.

duck breasts with peaches and tarragon

SERVES 4

Two 1-lb. boneless duck breasts
Kosher salt and freshly ground black pepper
1 Tbs. unsalted butter
2 medium shallots, thinly sliced (½ cup)
6 Tbs. dry white wine or dry vermouth
6 Tbs. lower-salt chicken broth
3 medium peaches (or 6 medium apricots), pitted and sliced ½ inch thick
1 Tbs. chopped fresh tarragon leaves
2 tsp. mild honey, such as clover honey

Position a rack in the center of the oven and heat the oven to 425°F. Score the skin and fat on each breast without cutting into the meat. Season with ½ tsp. salt and ½ tsp. pepper.

Heat a 12-inch ovenproof skillet over medium heat. Add the breasts skin side down and cook until the skin is browned and crisp, about 6 minutes. Flip and put the skillet in the oven. Roast until an instant-read thermometer inserted in the center registers 130° to 135°F for medium rare, 8 to 9 minutes.

Transfer the duck to a cutting board. Discard all but 1 Tbs. fat from the skillet. Swirl in the butter

tip

Don't wash peaches until you're ready to use them or they're likely to develop mold.

and return the skillet to medium heat. Add the shallots and cook, stirring often, until softened, about 2 minutes. Add the wine and simmer until reduced by half, about 2 minutes. Add the broth and simmer until reduced by half, another 2 minutes. Add the peaches, tarragon, honey, ½ tsp. salt, and ½ tsp. pepper. Stir until the sauce is bubbling, 1 minute.

Slice the duck and serve with the fruit sauce.

rigatoni with summer squash, spicy sausage & goat cheese

SERVES 4 TO 6

Kosher salt and freshly ground black pepper

1 lb. dried rigatoni

3 Tbs. extra-virgin olive oil

¾ lb. bulk hot Italian sausage (or links, casings removed)

⅓ cup finely chopped shallots (about 3 medium)

2 cups ¾-inch-diced yellow and green summer squash

3 oz. fresh goat cheese, crumbled (about ¾ cup)

2 tsp. finely chopped fresh flat-leaf parsley

¼ cup grated Parmigiano-Reggiano (optional)

Bring a large pot of well-salted water to a boil over high heat. Put the rigatoni in the boiling water and cook until just shy of al dente, about 10 minutes.

While the pasta cooks, heat ½ Tbs. of the oil in a 12-inch skillet over medium-high heat. Add the sausage and cook, breaking it into pieces with a spatula or spoon, until it's almost cooked through, 3 to 5 minutes. Using a slotted spoon, transfer the sausage to a bowl. Pour the fat out of the skillet but do not wipe it clean. Heat the remaining 2½ Tbs. oil in the skillet over medium heat and cook the shallots until they begin to soften, about 1 minute. Raise the heat to medium high and add the squash. Cook, stirring frequently, until the squash is barely tender, 3 to 5 minutes.

Reserve ½ cup of the pasta-cooking water and drain the rigatoni. Return the rigatoni to its cooking pot and add the sausage, the squash mixture, and 2 Tbs. of the reserved pasta water. Toss over medium heat until the sausage is cooked through and the rigatoni is perfectly al dente, about 3 minutes. Add more of the pasta water as necessary to keep the dish moist.

Remove from the heat, add the goat cheese and parsley, and toss until the cheese melts and coats the pasta. Season to taste with salt and pepper, transfer to warm shallow bowls, and top each serving with some of the grated Parmigiano, if using.

shrimp and vegetables with ginger-orange dressing

SERVES 4

½ lb. mizuna, washed and dried

⅓ cup plus 2 Tbs. vegetable oil

2 cloves garlic, chopped

2 tsp. chopped fresh ginger

½ red onion, thinly sliced

1 cup sliced shiitake mushroom caps (6 medium)

1 small red bell pepper, cored, seeded, and julienned

¼ lb. snow peas, cut in half if large

24 jumbo shrimp (16 to 20 per lb.), peeled and deveined

2 Tbs. rice vinegar

Juice and grated zest of 1 orange

1 Tbs. Thai sweet-hot chili sauce

1 tsp. chopped fresh cilantro

2 tsp. soy sauce

Divide the mizuna among four large serving plates or shallow bowls. Set aside.

In a large sauté pan, heat 2 Tbs. of the oil over high heat. Add the garlic and ginger; sauté lightly, about 15 seconds. Add the onion, shiitakes, bell pepper, and snow peas and sauté about 3 minutes. Add the peeled shrimp and sauté just until the shrimp begins to turn pink, about 2 minutes. Add the vinegar, orange juice, and zest, and turn off the heat. Add the remaining ⅓ cup oil, the chili sauce, cilantro, and soy sauce; stir to combine. With a slotted spoon, distribute the shrimp and vegetables over the mizuna. Drizzle the dressing over each portion and serve immediately.

summer squash pasta "carbonara"

SERVES 4 TO 6

Kosher salt and freshly ground black
  pepper
5 slices bacon, cut crosswise into
  ½-inch pieces
3 Tbs. extra-virgin olive oil
2 Tbs. finely chopped shallots
1 lb. summer squash (about
  3 medium), halved lengthwise and
  sliced into ¼-inch-thick half-moons

2 Tbs. thinly sliced fresh basil;
  more for serving
1 cup whole milk ricotta,
  at room temperature
1 lb. linguine
1 oz. Parmigiano-Reggiano, coarsely
  grated (½ cup); more for serving

Bring a large pot of well-salted water to a boil.

In a 12-inch nonstick skillet, cook the bacon over medium heat, stirring, until crisp, about 8 minutes. Pour off all but 1 Tbs. of fat, then add 2 Tbs. oil and the shallots and cook until they turn golden, about 1 minute. Add the squash; cook, stirring occasionally, until lightly browned and tender, about 7 minutes. Stir in the basil and ¾ tsp. salt; remove from the heat.

Mix the ricotta and the remaining 1 Tbs. oil in a medium bowl. Season well with pepper.

Boil the linguine according to the package instructions until al dente. Reserve 1 cup of the pasta water; drain the pasta and add it to the squash. Add the ricotta and Parmigiano and toss to combine, adding some of the cooking water to loosen the sauce, if necessary. Season to taste with salt and pepper, and serve garnished with basil and cheese.

fresh tagliatelle with sausage, red peppers & arugula

SERVES 4

Kosher salt and freshly ground black
  pepper
2 Tbs. extra-virgin olive oil
8 oz. hot or sweet Italian sausage,
  casings removed
2 medium cloves garlic, minced
One 13-oz. jar roasted red peppers,
  drained and finely chopped
  (1¾ cups)
½ cup heavy cream

One 10-oz. package fresh tagliatelle
  or fettuccine
4 cups loosely packed baby arugula
  (about 2½ oz.)
¾ oz. (½ cup) freshly grated
  Parmigiano-Reggiano
8 large fresh basil leaves, thinly
  sliced (optional)

Bring a large pot of well-salted water to a boil over
high heat.

   Meanwhile, heat the olive oil in a 12-inch
skillet over medium heat. Break the sausage
into bite-size pieces and add them to the skillet.
Cook, stirring frequently, until browned, about
4 minutes. Pour off all but 1 Tbs. of the fat and
return the skillet to medium heat. Add the garlic
and cook for 30 seconds. Add the peppers

tip

Hot Italian
sausage will
make this dish
spicy; for less heat,
use sweet sausage.

and cream and bring to a simmer. Reduce the heat to low and simmer gently until the sauce is slightly thickened, 8 minutes.

Cook the pasta in the boiling water according to the package instructions. Drain well and transfer to a large serving bowl. Add the sauce, arugula, cheese, and basil (if using) and toss with tongs until the arugula is slightly wilted. Season to taste with salt and pepper and serve.

grilled chicken and summer squash salad

SERVES 4

1 large clove garlic, mashed to a paste with ½ tsp. kosher salt

¾ cup canola oil

¼ cup fresh lime juice and 2 tsp. finely grated zest (from 1 lime)

¼ cup chopped fresh cilantro leaves and tender stems

1 ½ Tbs. finely grated peeled fresh ginger

1 Tbs. finely chopped jalapeño (seeded if you like; about ½ jalapeño)

1 tsp. granulated sugar

Kosher salt and freshly ground black pepper

1½ to 1¾ lb. mixed summer squash, such as zucchini, yellow zucchini, and yellow squash, sliced ¾ inch thick on an extreme angle (about 3 medium)

1½ lb. boneless, skinless chicken breast halves, pounded to an even thickness

5 oz. baby arugula

Heat a gas grill to medium high or prepare a medium-hot charcoal fire.

Put the garlic paste, oil, lime juice and zest, cilantro, ginger, jalapeño, sugar, and 1 tsp. salt in a small jar with a lid. Shake to emulsify.

Put the squash and chicken on a rimmed baking sheet, drizzle with ½ cup of the vinaigrette, and toss to coat. Grill on both sides until the squash is barely tender and the chicken is just cooked through, 4 to 6 minutes total. Transfer to a cutting board and let cool briefly.

Meanwhile, toss the arugula in a large bowl with ¼ cup of the vinaigrette and season with a pinch of salt and pepper. Divide among four plates.

Cut the squash and chicken into bite-size pieces. Put them in the bowl and toss with the remaining vinaigrette and sprinkle with salt and pepper to taste. Use a slotted spoon to divide the mixture among the plates.

tip

After a gentle scrub, there's no need to peel summer squash. Its skin is thin and mild-flavored. Besides contributing color and nutrients, the skin helps the vegetable hold together better when cooked.

flat iron steak with zucchini, edamame & soba noodles

SERVES 6

Kosher salt
8 oz. dried soba noodles
1 Tbs. Asian sesame oil
¾ cup soy sauce
¾ cup mirin
¼ cup granulated sugar
Three ¼-inch-thick slices peeled
   fresh ginger
2 medium cloves garlic, peeled
2 flat iron steaks (8 to 10 oz. each)
1 lb. zucchini (2 medium), cut into
   2-inch matchsticks

One 12-oz. bag frozen shelled
   edamame, thawed (about 2 cups)
1 Tbs. chopped pickled ginger
   (optional)
2 small scallions (white and
   light-green parts), thinly sliced
   (optional)
1 Tbs. toasted sesame seeds
   (optional)

Bring a large pot of well-salted water to a boil and cook the noodles until tender, about 4 minutes. Drain well, transfer to a large bowl, toss with the sesame oil, cover, and keep warm.

Meanwhile, combine the soy sauce, mirin, sugar, ginger, garlic, and 1 cup water in a 10-inch straight-sided sauté pan. Bring to a boil, and then add the steaks. Turn the heat down and simmer gently, flipping once, until medium rare (130°F), 12 to 16 minutes. Transfer the steaks to a cutting board, reserving the liquid in the pan. Discard the garlic and ginger.

Return the liquid to a boil. Add the zucchini and edamame, return to a boil, and then lower to a simmer. Cook until the vegetables are just tender, about 2 minutes. Using a slotted spoon, transfer the vegetables to the bowl of noodles. Toss well, cover, and keep warm.

Boil the cooking liquid until reduced by half, about 5 minutes.

Thinly slice the steaks across the grain. Arrange the noodle mixture on a platter or divide it among six shallow bowls. Top with the beef and the pickled ginger, if using. Drizzle some of the sauce over the beef and garnish with the scallions and sesame seeds, if using. Serve, passing the rest of the sauce at the table.

tip

The deep flavor of flat iron steak works really well with the umami-rich soy sauce and sesame oil featured in this dish. If you can't find flat iron, substitute rib-eye.

warm shrimp salad with honeydew and feta

SERVES 4

1½ lb. jumbo (16 to 20 per lb.) shrimp, peeled (tails left on, if you like) and deveined

Kosher salt and freshly ground black pepper

Pinch of cayenne

¼ cup extra-virgin olive oil

2 Tbs. finely chopped shallots

1 medium lime, finely grated to yield 1 tsp. zest, squeezed to yield 4 tsp. juice

2 heads frisée (about ½ lb.), torn into bite-size pieces

1 medium (3- to 4-lb.) honeydew melon, peeled, seeded, and cut into ½-inch dice (about 4 cups)

8 oz. feta, crumbled (about 1½ cups)

¼ cup thinly sliced fresh mint

1 Tbs. plus 1 tsp. cracked coriander seeds

Season the shrimp lightly with salt and cayenne.

In a 12-inch skillet, heat 2 Tbs. of the oil over medium-high heat until shimmering hot. Add the shrimp and cook on one side until pink, about 1 minute. Flip and add the shallots, lime zest, and 1 tsp. of the lime juice. Turn the heat to medium and cook until just opaque throughout, about 1 minute more.

In a large bowl, whisk the remaining 2 Tbs. oil and 1 Tbs. lime juice. Season to taste with salt and pepper. Toss the frisée and the melon in the vinaigrette. Divide equally among four dinner plates, top with the shrimp, feta, mint, and coriander and serve.

pan-seared tuna steaks with warm tomato, basil & olive salad

SERVES 4

Four 5-oz. boneless, skinless tuna
   steaks
Kosher salt and freshly ground
   black pepper
2 Tbs. extra-virgin olive oil
1 medium shallot, finely chopped

2 cups mixed yellow and red grape
   or cherry tomatoes, halved
⅓ cup sliced pitted green olives,
   such as picholine or Cerignola
2 Tbs. finely chopped fresh basil
½ Tbs. fresh lemon juice

Season the tuna with 1 tsp. salt and ¼ tsp. pepper. Heat the oil in a 12-inch skillet over medium-high heat. Arrange the tuna in the skillet in a single layer and cook, turning once, until done to your liking (3 to 4 minutes for medium rare). Transfer the tuna to a large plate.

Reduce the heat to medium and add the shallots to the skillet. Cook, stirring, until golden-brown, about 1 minute. Add the tomatoes, olives, basil, ½ tsp. salt, and a few grinds of pepper; cook until warmed through and the tomatoes are just softened, about 2 minutes more. Remove the skillet from the heat and gently stir in the lemon juice.

Transfer the tuna to plates, top with the tomato salad, and serve.

cucumber and feta toss with mint and dill

SERVES 6

2 medium seedless English
  cucumbers (about 1½ lb.)
4 oz. feta, crumbled (scant 1 cup)
One-half medium sweet onion (such
  as Vidalia, Maui, or Walla Walla),
  sliced lengthwise as thinly as
  possible

¼ cup chopped fresh mint
¼ cup chopped fresh dill
2 Tbs. extra-virgin olive oil
2 Tbs. fresh lemon juice
Kosher salt and freshly ground
  black pepper
Mint leaves for garnish (optional)

Trim the ends of the cucumbers. With a vegetable peeler, peel them in ½-inch intervals, leaving ½-inch strips of peel intact. Halve the cucumbers lengthwise, scoop out and discard the core, and then cut them into ¾-inch dice.

In a large bowl, combine the cucumbers, feta, onion, mint, and dill.

In a small bowl, whisk the olive oil and lemon juice and season to taste with salt and pepper. Gently toss the dressing with the cucumber mixture. Season to taste with salt and pepper, garnish with the mint leaves (if using), and serve.

mexican grilled corn on the cob

SERVES 4

4 ears fresh corn, husks and silks
   removed
¼ cup mayonnaise
½ Tbs. Mexican-style chili powder

½ tsp. finely grated lime zest
¼ cup crumbled Cotija cheese
   (or ricotta salata)
Lime wedges, for serving

Heat a gas grill to high or prepare a hot charcoal fire. Grill the corn, turning frequently with tongs, until charred in spots, 6 to 8 minutes.

In a small bowl, combine the mayonnaise, chili powder, and lime zest. Put the Cotija on a small plate. Spread each ear of corn with 1 Tbs. of the mayonnaise and then roll in the cheese to coat. Sprinkle with kosher salt and serve with lime wedges for squeezing over the corn.

tip

Cotija is an aged, crumbly, slightly salty Mexican cheese traditionally made from cow's milk. The texture is somewhat akin to feta. Look for Cotija in Latin American grocery stores.

slow-roasted tomatoes

YIELDS ABOUT 3 CUPS

4 lb. ripe, meaty tomatoes, such
as beefsteak or plum, cored and
sliced crosswise ½ inch thick
2 medium cloves garlic, smashed
and peeled

½ cup extra-virgin olive oil
Kosher salt and freshly ground black
pepper

Position racks in the upper and lower thirds of
the oven and heat the oven to 350°F.

Divide the tomatoes and garlic between
two large rimmed baking sheets. Drizzle the oil
over the tomatoes and season with 1 tsp. salt
and several grinds of pepper. Gently toss the
tomatoes to evenly coat with the oil and then
spread in a single layer.

Put the sheets in the oven and lower the heat
to 225°F. Slowly roast, switching the positions of
the sheets halfway through, until the tomatoes
look like juicy sun-dried tomatoes, wrinkly and
slightly browned in spots, 5 to 6 hours. Let the
tomatoes cool for at least 10 minutes before
serving or using.

tip

✛ The tomatoes
can be refrig-
erated in an airtight
container for up to
1 week or frozen for
up to 2 months.

haricots verts with toasted walnuts and goat cheese

SERVES 4

Kosher salt and freshly ground black pepper
¾ lb. haricots verts (green, yellow, or both), trimmed
1 Tbs. extra-virgin olive oil
2 Tbs. minced shallots

⅓ cup walnuts, lightly toasted and chopped
2 tsp. walnut oil
2 oz. fresh goat cheese, crumbled (⅔ cup)

Bring a medium pot of well-salted water to a boil. Cook the beans in the water until tender, 2 to 3 minutes. Drain and run under cold water to cool. Drain well.

Heat the olive oil in a 12-inch skillet over medium-high heat. Add the shallots and cook, stirring, until they begin to brown, about 30 seconds. Stir in the walnuts. Add the walnut oil and the beans and cook, stirring to heat through, 2 to 3 minutes. Season to taste with salt and pepper and transfer the beans to a serving dish. Sprinkle the goat cheese over the top and serve.

herb-roasted potatoes and onions

SERVES 6

¼ cup extra-virgin olive oil; more for the baking sheet
2 lb. small (about 1½-inch) potatoes, halved
Kosher salt
2 Tbs. coarsely chopped mixed hardy fresh herbs, such as rosemary, savory, and thyme

1 large onion, halved lengthwise and thinly sliced
½ cup coarsely chopped mixed tender fresh herbs, such as chives, parsley, and tarragon
Flaky sea salt, for serving (optional)

Position a rack in the center of the oven and heat the oven to 450°F. Oil a large rimmed baking sheet.

In a medium bowl, toss the potatoes with the olive oil and 1 tsp. salt to coat.

Sprinkle the hardy herbs over the bottom of the baking sheet, spread the onion slices over the herbs, and top with the potatoes, cut side down. Scrape any olive oil remaining in the bowl over the potatoes.

Roast until the potatoes are tender and brown on the edges, 30 to 35 minutes. Transfer the potatoes and onions to a bowl and toss with the tender herbs. Season to taste with sea salt, if using, or kosher salt and serve.

dill garden pickles

MAKES ABOUT 2 QUARTS

1¼ cups white-wine vinegar
2 Tbs. mustard seed
1 Tbs. coriander seed
2 tsp. celery seed
2 tsp. black peppercorns
1 tsp. caraway seed
3 dried bay leaves, crumbled
1⅛ oz. kosher salt (3 Tbs. Diamond Crystal® or 2 Tbs. Morton®)

8 cups of the following vegetables, in any combination you like: pickling cucumbers, such as Kirby, cut into spears; green beans, ends trimmed; celery, cut into 2-inch pieces; carrots, peeled, halved lengthwise, and cut into 3- to 4-inch pieces; bell peppers, seeded and cut lengthwise into strips or crosswise into rings; green tomatoes or tomatillos, quartered
¼ cup chopped fresh dill
¼ cup finely chopped garlic (about 8 large cloves)

In a 2- to 3-quart nonreactive saucepan, bring the vinegar, spices, salt, and 3¼ cups water to a simmer over medium heat, stirring until the salt dissolves. Simmer over low heat for 5 to 7 minutes to meld the flavors. Let cool to room temperature, about 1 hour.

Pack the vegetables, dill, and garlic into two 1-quart jars or other sealable nonreactive container.

Cover the vegetables with the liquid. Let sit, uncovered, at room temperature for 2 hours to pickle the vegetables. Serve, or cover and refrigerate for up to 3 weeks.

roasted eggplant with chiles, peanuts & mint

SERVES 4 TO 6

¼ cup unsalted peanuts

5 Tbs. plus 1 tsp. peanut oil

Kosher salt

4 skinny Japanese eggplant
(about 7 inches long and 1½ inches
in diameter)

¼ tsp. crushed red pepper flakes;
more to taste

2 Tbs. fresh lime juice

1 tsp. honey

12 medium fresh mint leaves,
coarsely torn (about 3 Tbs.)

Position a rack in the center of the oven and heat the oven to 425°F.

Scatter the peanuts in a pie plate or other small baking dish and toss them with 1 tsp. oil and a generous pinch of salt. Roast, shaking the pan once or twice, until they are golden-brown, about 5 minutes. Set aside to cool, and then coarsely chop them. Reduce the oven temperature to 375°F.

Rinse the eggplant. Trim off their tops and then cut the eggplant in half lengthwise. In a large, shallow bowl, toss the eggplant with 2 Tbs. of the oil and the red pepper flakes. Put the eggplant cut side up on a rimmed baking sheet and sprinkle generously with salt. Roast until the eggplant is tender when pierced with a fork and the flesh is a light golden brown, 10 to 12 minutes.

Meanwhile, in a small dish, whisk the remaining 3 Tbs. oil with the lime juice, honey, and ¼ tsp. salt. Season to taste with more salt, if necessary.

With the eggplant still on the center rack, turn the broiler on to high and broil the eggplant until well browned on top, about 5 minutes. Transfer the eggplant to a serving platter. Drizzle with the dressing. Sprinkle with mint and peanuts and serve.

tip

✦ Japanese eggplant has tender skin and a soft, creamy flesh. It's less bitter than large globe eggplant, so it doesn't need to be salted before cooking. Also, because this skinny variety is small and firm, it cooks faster and doesn't need as much oil as larger eggplants.

roasted squash with pimentón and manchego

SERVES 4

1½ lbs. assorted summer squash, cut
　into 1-inch chunks
1 tsp. kosher salt
1 cup medium-diced yellow onion

1 Tbs. extra-virgin olive oil
1½ tsp. hot pimentón
1 cup coarsely grated manchego

Position a rack in the center of the oven and heat the oven to 450°F. In a colander, toss the squash with the salt and drain for 30 minutes; transfer to a large bowl.

　　Toss the squash with the onion, olive oil, and hot pimentón. Arrange in single layer on a rimmed baking sheet. Roast until the squash is lightly golden, about 20 minutes, then flip and continue to roast until the squash and onion are golden-brown and tender, about 20 minutes more. Sprinkle with the manchego, toss gently, and serve.

tip

For variety, use different types of squash, like zucchini and pattypan.

grilled onions with thyme and cream

SERVES 4

3 medium yellow or red onions (or a mix), trimmed, peeled, and sliced crosswise into ½-inch-thick rounds (12 slices total)
Olive oil, for brushing

Kosher salt and freshly ground black pepper
½ cup heavy cream
1 tsp. minced garlic
1 tsp. chopped fresh thyme

Position a rack in the center of the oven and heat the oven to 350°F.

Heat a gas grill to medium or prepare a medium-hot charcoal fire. Brush the onion slices with oil and season with salt and pepper.

Grill the onion slices until grill marks form on one side, 7 to 8 minutes. Flip the slices and continue to grill until tender, 7 to 8 minutes more. Stack the onions on a large piece of foil, wrap them up, and let them sit for 10 minutes to soften further.

In a small bowl, combine the cream, garlic, thyme, ¼ tsp. salt, and ¼ tsp. pepper.

Arrange the onion slices in a snug single layer in 1 large or 2 small shallow baking dishes. Drizzle with the cream mixture. Bake until hot, about 10 minutes.

spanish-style grilled pepper potato salad

SERVES 6

3 red, yellow, or orange bell peppers (or a mix), quartered lengthwise, stemmed, and seeded
Olive oil, for brushing
Kosher salt and freshly ground black pepper

2 lb. red or yellow baby potatoes, halved (or quartered if large)
½ cup mayonnaise
2 Tbs. chopped fresh flat-leaf parsley
1 Tbs. minced garlic

Heat a gas grill to medium high or prepare a medium-hot charcoal fire. Brush the pepper quarters with oil and season with salt and pepper.

Put the potatoes in a 4-quart pot with 1 tsp. kosher salt and enough cool water to cover. Boil over high heat, partially covered, until just tender, about 8 minutes. Drain and transfer to a large bowl.

Meanwhile, grill the peppers skin side down until grill marks form on one side, about 5 minutes. Flip the peppers and continue to grill until crisp-tender, about 2 minutes more. Let the peppers cool slightly, then cut into bite-size pieces and add to the potatoes.

In a small bowl, combine the mayonnaise, parsley, and garlic. Add to the potato mixture and toss to coat. Season to taste with salt and pepper. Serve warm or at room temperature.

shredded carrots with jalapeño, lime & cilantro

SERVES 6

8 medium carrots (about 1½ lb.)
¼ cup extra-virgin olive oil
3 Tbs. fresh lime juice
1 medium jalapeño, cored, seeded, and minced
Kosher salt and freshly ground black pepper

½ cup coarsely chopped fresh cilantro
Whole cilantro leaves for garnish (optional)

Peel and then grate the carrots using either the large holes on a box grater or in a food processor fitted with a medium grating attachment. Put the grated carrots in a large bowl.

In a small bowl, whisk the oil and lime juice. Add the jalapeño and season to taste with salt and pepper.

Add the dressing and chopped cilantro to the carrots and toss. Season to taste with salt and pepper, garnish with the cilantro leaves (if using), and serve.

bread-and-butter pickles

MAKES ABOUT 2½ QUARTS

3 lb. pickling cucumbers, such as Kirby, trimmed and sliced ¼ inch thick (about 9 cups)
1 medium yellow or white onion, halved and thinly sliced
Kosher salt (¼ cup Diamond Crystal or 2 Tbs. plus 2 tsp. Morton)
3 cups cider vinegar
2¼ cups packed light brown sugar
1 Tbs. yellow mustard seed
1 tsp. celery seed
1 tsp. ground turmeric

In a large bowl, toss the cucumbers and onion with the salt until thoroughly mixed. Refrigerate, covered, for 1 to 2 hours.

Quickly rinse and drain, then use your hands to squeeze out any excess moisture. Divide among three 1-quart jars or other sealable nonreactive containers.

In a 2- to 3-quart nonreactive saucepan, bring the vinegar, brown sugar, mustard seed, celery seed, and turmeric to a simmer over medium heat, stirring until the sugar dissolves, 3 to 5 minutes.

Pour the liquid and spices over the vegetables to cover by an inch or more. Let sit, uncovered, at room temperature until cool, about 2 hours. Serve, or cover and refrigerate for up to 2 months.

tip

These sweet and sour pickles can be eaten as soon as they cool, but the longer they sit, the more flavorful and crunchy they'll become.

watermelon and tea granita

SERVES 8

¼ vanilla bean
1 Tbs. good-quality loose black tea,
   such as English Breakfast
⅔ cup boiling water
2 Tbs. granulated sugar
3 cups puréed watermelon
   (from about 4 cups diced,
   seeded watermelon)

1 Tbs. fresh lemon juice
Kosher salt
Sweetened whipped cream
   (optional)

Split the vanilla bean and scrape out the seeds. Put the vanilla seeds and tea in a small bowl (save the pod for another use). Add the boiling water and steep for 10 minutes. Add the sugar and stir gently to dissolve.

In a large bowl, combine the watermelon purée, lemon juice, and ¼ tsp. salt. Strain the tea mixture into the watermelon mixture and stir to combine. Pour into a 9x9-inch metal baking pan, cover with plastic wrap, and freeze. After 1 hour, stir and scrape the mixture with a fork, repeating every 30 to 40 minutes, until the mixture has an icy shard-like consistency, about 3½ hours total.

To serve, scrape the granita into chilled bowls and top with a dollop of sweetened whipped cream (if using).

peach and blueberry crisp with spiced-pecan topping

SERVES 6

4 Tbs. unsalted butter, softened; more for the pan
⅔ cup all-purpose flour
½ cup packed light brown sugar
½ tsp. ground cinnamon
¼ tsp. table salt
⅔ cup coarsely chopped pecans

3 cups (about 1 lb.) room-temperature blueberries, washed and drained on paper towels
3 medium peaches (about 1 lb.), halved, pitted, and sliced ½ inch thick
¼ cup granulated sugar
3 Tbs. cornstarch
¼ tsp. freshly ground nutmeg

Position a rack in the center of the oven and heat the oven to 375°F. Lightly butter a 9-inch square metal or ceramic baking pan.

In a small bowl, combine the flour, brown sugar, cinnamon, and ⅛ tsp. of the salt. With your fingers, work the butter into the flour mixture until the mixture readily clumps together when pressed. Mix in the pecans.

In a large bowl, toss the blueberries and peaches. In a small bowl, combine the granulated sugar with the cornstarch, nutmeg, and the remaining ⅛ tsp. salt and toss this mixture with the fruit.

Spread the fruit into the prepared pan, then sprinkle the streusel over the fruit. Bake until the fruit is bubbling in the center and the topping is crisp and well browned, 45 to 50 minutes. Serve warm.

eton mess

SERVES 6 TO 8

2 cups chilled heavy cream
2 Tbs. granulated sugar
1 lb. strawberries, hulled (about 4 cups)
2 Tbs. plus 1 tsp. strawberry eau de vie or kirsch
2 oz. meringue cookies, crumbled into ½- to ¾-inch pieces

Place the cream and sugar in a blender and blend until the cream just forms stiff peaks, about 10 seconds.

Add 3 cups of the strawberries to the blender along with 2 Tbs. of the eau de vie and blend briefly until the strawberries are incorporated but still chunky, about 5 seconds.

Divide three-quarters of the meringue crumbles among six to eight glass dessert dishes. Top evenly with the strawberry cream. Slice the remaining 1 cup strawberries and toss with the remaining 1 tsp. eau de vie. Spoon the sliced berries on top of the strawberry cream and sprinkle with the remaining meringue cookies.

tip

Named after a prestigious English boarding school, this mash-up of strawberries, whipped cream, and meringue crumbles is served at an annual cricket match there.

blackberry fool

SERVES 4

1½ cups fresh blackberries
1 chipotle chile (from a can of
   chipotles in adobo sauce),
   stemmed
3 Tbs. light brown sugar

1 tsp. fresh lime juice
1 cup heavy cream
1½ Tbs. confectioners' sugar
½ tsp. pure vanilla extract

Set a medium-mesh sieve over a medium bowl. Use the back of a wooden spoon to push 1 cup of the blackberries and the chipotle through the sieve, smearing the berries and chile back and forth across the mesh until only seeds and pulp remain. Scrape any purée from the bottom of the sieve. Stir the brown sugar and lime juice into the purée.

In a chilled medium metal bowl, combine the cream, confectioners' sugar, and vanilla and beat with an electric hand-held mixer on high speed until soft peaks form, about 2 minutes.

Pour the blackberry mixture over the cream. Use a butter knife to gently stir the mixture so that thin streaks of dark purple run through the cream.

Spoon the mixture into four glasses or small dessert bowls and top with the remaining blackberries.

blackberry-orange ice pops

MAKES ABOUT TEN 1⅓-CUP POPS

½ cup granulated sugar
Pinch of kosher salt
1 Tbs. loose black tea leaves

4 cups blackberries
1 cup orange segments, cut free of
    their membranes and halved

Combine the sugar, salt, and ½ cup water in a 2-quart saucepan over medium heat. Bring to a boil and make sure the sugar has dissolved; add the tea leaves. Reduce the heat to medium low and simmer for 2 minutes. Remove from the heat and let the syrup cool completely. Strain through a fine-mesh strainer into a 1-quart liquid measuring cup, and discard the solids in the strainer.

Purée the berries in batches in a blender and strain if you like. Measure out 2 cups (save extra for another use); combine with the syrup.

Distribute the orange segments among ten ⅓-cup pop molds. Add the fruit mixture to each mold, leaving about ¼ inch at the top to allow for expansion. Stir gently with a Popsicle® stick to distribute the orange segments. Freeze until partially frozen, about 1 hour. Insert the sticks and freeze again until the pops are fully set, 4 to 6 hours more.

To unmold, dip the mold in a deep pan of hot water until the pops pull out easily, 30 to 40 seconds, or let sit at room temperature for 5 to 10 minutes. Unmold and store the pops in individual resealable plastic bags; they're best eaten within 3 weeks.

warm berries and nectarines with mascarpone

SERVES 3 TO 4

2 Tbs. granulated sugar
1 tsp. ground ginger
4 cups ripe mixed berries
   (such as raspberries, blueberries,
   and blackberries)

3 medium ripe nectarines,
   thinly sliced
¼ cup mascarpone
   (or Greek yogurt)

In a large (12-inch) skillet, combine the sugar and ginger with ⅓ cup water and put the pan over medium-high heat. When the water comes to a boil, add the berries and nectarines and cook, stirring frequently, until the nectarines have just started to soften and the juice released from the berries has thickened slightly, 4 to 5 minutes. Let cool for a minute and then transfer to individual serving bowls and garnish with a dollop of mascarpone.

summer fruit cobbler

SERVES 6 TO 8

8 Tbs. unsalted butter, cut into
    8 pieces
1 cup unbleached all-purpose flour
1 cup granulated sugar
1½ tsp. baking powder
Pinch of kosher salt
1 cup whole milk

3 cups mixed whole or sliced
    fresh summer fruit, such as
    blackberries, blueberries,
    raspberries, peaches, plums, and
    nectarines
Vanilla ice cream, for serving

Position a rack in the center of the oven and heat the oven to 375°F.
Put the butter in 3-quart baking dish or similar, or in a 10- to 12-inch
ovenproof skillet and put the dish or pan in the oven to melt the butter
while the oven is heating.

Meanwhile, stir or whisk the flour, sugar, baking powder, and salt in
a medium bowl until well combined. Add the milk and stir or whisk until
combined; a few small lumps are OK.

When the butter is fully melted, take the baking dish out of the oven
and pour the batter over the melted butter; do not mix. Scatter the fruit
over the batter, favoring the middle of the dish more than the edges; do
not mix it in. Bake until the top is a rich golden-brown, 30 to 45 minutes.
Serve warm with vanilla ice cream.

apple-blackberry crisp

SERVES 6 TO 8

For the topping
1 cup unbleached all-purpose flour
½ cup packed dark brown sugar
¼ cup granulated sugar
Pinch of kosher salt
½ tsp. ground cinnamon
8 Tbs. slightly softened unsalted
    butter, cut into pieces
⅓ cup chopped hazelnuts

For the filling
4 cups sliced apples (½-inch slices)
2 cups blackberries
2 Tbs. to ⅓ cup sugar, depending on
    the sweetness of the fruit
2 tsp. cornstarch
1 Tbs. lemon juice

Position a rack in the center of the oven and heat the oven to 375°F.

Make the topping

Combine the flour, both sugars, salt, and cinnamon in a medium bowl. Rub in the butter with your fingertips until it's well blended and the mixture crumbles coarsely; it should hold together when you pinch it. Add the hazelnuts. Refrigerate the topping until you're ready to use it.

Make the filling

Put the apples and blackberries in a large bowl. Taste the fruit and sprinkle on the sugar as needed (use 2 Tbs. sugar for very ripe fruit, or up to ⅓ cup for more tart, less-ripe fruit).

    In a small dish, dissolve the cornstarch in the lemon juice. Gently toss the mixture with the fruit.

Make the crisp

Pour the fruit into an 8- or 9-inch square (or similar-capacity) glass or ceramic baking dish. Set the pan on a baking sheet to catch overflowing juices. Top the fruit with half of the topping (keep the other half refrigerated) and bake for 20 minutes.

Sprinkle the remaining topping over the crisp and continue baking until the fruit is tender when pierced with a knife, the topping is crisp, and the juices are bubbling, another 25 to 35 minutes. Let cool for 20 to 30 minutes. Serve warm.

red currant and ginger sorbet

SERVES 8

18 oz. (4 cups) red currants,
    unstemmed
1¾ cups granulated sugar
2 Tbs. ruby port, such as Sandeman®

1 Tbs. finely chopped fresh ginger
¼ tsp. kosher salt

In a 5- to 6-quart pot, combine the currants, sugar, port, ginger, and salt. Add 2 cups of water and bring to a boil over medium heat; cook, stirring occasionally, until most of the berries have burst, about 8 minutes. Take the pot off the heat and crush the berries with a potato masher. Pour the mixture into a large, fine-mesh sieve set over a large bowl and press on the solids with the back of a large spoon to obtain as much liquid as possible. Discard the solids.

Refrigerate the liquid for at least 2 hours and up to 24 (or quick-chill in a larger bowl of ice water). Pour the liquid into an ice cream maker and churn according to the manufacturer's directions. Transfer to an airtight container and chill in the freezer until firmed up, at least 4 hours.

The sorbet will keep in the freezer for up to 1 week.

Recipe Index

Spicy Shrimp with Ginger-Garlic Long
Beans, 35
Summer Squash Pasta "Carbonara," 45
Warm Shrimp Salad with Honeydew and
Feta, 52

Sides

Bread-and-Butter Pickles, 66
Cucumber and Feta Toss with Mint and
Dill, 54
Dill Garden Pickles, 59
Grilled Onions with Thyme and Cream,
63
Haricots Verts with Toasted Walnuts
and Goat Cheese, 57
Herb-Roasted Potatoes and Onions, 58
Mexican Grilled Corn on the Cob, 55
Roasted Eggplant with Chiles, Peanuts
& Mint, 60–61

Roasted Squash with Pimentón and
Manchego, 62
Shredded Carrots with Jalapeño, Lime
& Cilantro, 65
Slow-Roasted Tomatoes, 56
Spanish-Style Grilled Pepper Potato
Salad, 64

Desserts

Apple-Blackberry Crisp, 74–75
Blackberry Fool, 70
Blackberry-Orange Ice Pops, 71
Eton Mess, 69
Peach and Blueberry Crisp with Spiced-
Pecan Topping, 68
Red Currant and Ginger Sorbet, 76
Summer Fruit Cobbler, 73
Warm Berries and Nectarine with
Mascarpone, 72
Watermelon and Tea Granita, 67

COOK FRESH YEAR-ROUND

SPRING

FROM

FINE COOKING

from the editors and contributors
of *fine cooking*

The Taunton Press

The Taunton Press
Inspiration for hands-on living®

The Taunton Press, Inc., 63 South Main Street,
PO Box 5506, Newtown, CT 06470-5506
e-mail: tp@taunton.com

Copy editor: Nina Rhyd Whitnah
Indexer: Heidi Blough
Jacket/Cover design: Stacy Wakefield Forte
Interior design: Stacy Wakefield Forte

Recipes from: Jennifer Armentrout, Robin Asbell, John Ash, David Bonom, Ronne
Day, Maryellen Driscoll, Naomi Duguid, Mindy Fox, Fran Gage, Ellen Jackson,
Sara Jenkins, Alison Ehri Kreitler, Ruth Lively, Lori Longbotham, Barbara Lynch,
Deborah Madison, Ivy Manning, Susie Middleton, Diane Morgan, Jan Newberry,
Liz Pearson, Melissa Pellegrino, Laraine Perri, Julissa Roberts, Tony Rosenfeld,
Michael Ruhlman, Samantha Seneviratne, Kathleen Stewart, Adeena Sussman,
Bill Telepan, Annie Wayte, Shelley Wiseman

The following names/brands appearing in *Spring* are trademarks: Cointreau®,
Pepperidge Farm®, Squid®

Library of Congress Cataloging-in-Publication Data
CookFresh year-round : seasonal recipes from Fine cooking /author, editors of
  Fine cooking.
    pages cm
  Includes index.
  ISBN 978-1-63186-014-0
1. Seasonal cooking. 2. Cookbooks. lcgft I. Taunton's fine cooking. II. Title: Cook
  Fresh year-round.
  TX714.C65428 2015
  641.5'64--dc23

                                2014039388

Printed in China
10 9 8 7 6 5 4 3 2 1

spring

contents

spinach and tomatillo guacamole

SERVES 4

2 oz. (2 packed cups) baby spinach
1 Tbs. extra-virgin olive oil
2 medium tomatillos, husked and
   chopped
2 coarsely chopped medium Hass
   avocados

1 small tomato, chopped
½ cup finely chopped white onion
¼ cup coarsely chopped fresh
   cilantro
1 Tbs. fresh lime juice; more to taste
Kosher salt

In a food processor, pulse the spinach, oil, and tomatillos to a coarse purée. Pour off any liquid, and then transfer the mixture to a medium bowl. Stir in the avocados, tomato, onion, cilantro, lime juice, and 1½ tsp. salt. Season to taste with more lime juice and salt. Serve immediately.

shaved baby artichokes with lemon, arugula & parmigiano

SERVES 8

3 Tbs. fresh lemon juice

2 ½ Tbs. extra-virgin olive oil

1 tsp. finely grated lemon zest

Kosher salt and freshly ground black pepper

8 baby artichokes, trimmed but left whole

10 oz. baby arugula (12 cups)

1 cup loosely packed torn fresh basil leaves

6 oz. Parmigiano-Reggiano, thinly shaved (2 cups)

In a small bowl, whisk the lemon juice, oil, lemon zest, ½ tsp. salt, and ¼ tsp. pepper.

Blot the baby artichokes dry with a dishtowel. With a mandoline or food processor fitted with a 2mm slicing blade, very thinly slice the artichokes lengthwise. As you work, immediately return the artichoke slices to lemon water (juice of 2 lemons mixed in 2 to 3 quarts of water). When all the artichokes are sliced, drain, blot dry, and transfer the slices to a large bowl and toss with enough of the dressing to lightly coat (whisk first to recombine). Let sit for about 5 minutes. Toss in the arugula and basil.

Arrange the salad on a platter or individual serving plates and garnish with the shaved Parmigiano. Drizzle the remaining dressing over the salad and sprinkle with salt and pepper.

fava bean purée

YIELDS ABOUT 1½ CUPS

½ cup extra-virgin olive oil; more for drizzling
2 large cloves garlic, chopped
1 tsp. finely chopped fresh rosemary or thyme
Kosher salt and freshly ground black pepper
3 lb. fava beans, shelled and peeled, to yield 2 cups
2 Tbs. fresh lemon juice; more to taste

Put a 10-inch skillet over medium-high heat. Add ¼ cup of the oil, the garlic, rosemary or thyme, ½ tsp. salt, and ⅛ tsp. pepper and cook until you begin to hear a sizzling sound and the aromatics are fragrant, 1 to 2 minutes. Add the fava beans. Stir until the beans are well coated with the oil and aromatics and then add 1 cup of water. Bring to a boil, reduce the heat to medium, and cook until the water has nearly evaporated and the fava beans are tender, about 12 minutes. Add more water if the pan looks dry before the favas are done. Remove from the heat.

Transfer the fava mixture to a food processor. Add the remaining ¼ cup olive oil and the lemon juice and purée until smooth, stopping to scrape the bowl as needed. Season to taste with more salt and lemon juice. Drizzle with a little olive oil before serving as a dip or spread.

tip

This purée is terrific on crostini, but you can also use it as a dip for vegetables, pita chips, or bread.

deviled eggs with crabmeat and cayenne

YIELDS 8

4 large eggs
3 Tbs. mayonnaise
1 tsp. Dijon mustard
1 tsp. dry sherry
½ tsp. Worcestershire sauce
Big pinch cayenne

2 oz. crabmeat picked over and
   shredded (scant ¼ cup)
Kosher salt and freshly ground black
   pepper
Fresh lemon juice, to taste
Paprika for sprinkling (optional)

Prepare an ice water bath. Arrange the eggs in a single layer in a steamer basket set over boiling water. Cover the steamer with a tight-fitting lid and steam for 10 minutes. Turn off the heat and let the eggs sit, covered, for 5 minutes more.

Plunge the eggs into the ice bath. Working with one egg at a time, crack the shell by rolling it on a flat surface. Under a stream of cold running water, peel the shell.

Let the eggs come to room temperature, then slice in half lengthwise. Remove the yolks, transfer them to a small bowl, and mash them with the back of a spoon.

Add the mayonnaise, mustard, sherry, Worcestershire sauce, and cayenne and continue to mash until smooth. Gently stir in the crabmeat and season to taste with salt, pepper, and lemon juice. Pipe or spoon equal amounts of the mixture into the hollows of the egg whites. When ready to serve, sprinkle with a little paprika, if you wish.

rhubarb chutney

MAKES ABOUT 2½ CUPS

⅓ cup cider vinegar
2 bay leaves
1½ tsp. coriander seeds, lightly crushed
1 tsp. fennel seeds, lightly crushed
1 cinnamon stick
Kosher salt and freshly ground black pepper
3 Tbs. canola or other neutral-flavored oil
3 large shallots, halved lengthwise and thinly sliced crosswise (1 heaping cup)
1 Tbs. yellow mustard seeds
¼ tsp. crushed red pepper flakes
⅔ cup mild honey
¾ lb. rhubarb, trimmed and cut into ½-inch pieces (about 2½ cups)
½ cup golden raisins

In a 3-quart pot, combine the vinegar, bay leaves, coriander seeds, fennel seeds, cinnamon, and 1 tsp. salt; bring to a simmer over medium-high heat. Remove from the heat, cover the pot, and let sit for 15 minutes for the flavors to develop.

Meanwhile, heat the oil in a 10-inch skillet over medium heat. Add the shallots, mustard seeds, and red pepper flakes and cook, stirring, until softened, about 5 minutes.

Stir the shallot mixture and the honey into the vinegar and bring to a simmer. Cover and simmer for about 5 minutes to combine the flavors. Remove the bay leaves and cinnamon

tip

If the stalk is very large, you may want to peel away the outer layer in case it's stringy, but that's not usually necessary. Serve the chutney as part of a cheese course.

stick. Add the rhubarb and raisins and stir to combine. Cover and cook over low heat, without stirring, until the rhubarb is tender and starting to fall apart, about 10 minutes. Season to taste with salt and black pepper. Transfer to a serving dish and cool to room temperature. The chutney will keep, covered and refrigerated, for 2 weeks. Serve cool or at room temperature.

spinach and mushroom salad with miso-tahini dressing

SERVES 4

¼ cup tahini
3 Tbs. fresh lemon juice
2 Tbs. white miso
½ tsp. sweet paprika
½ tsp. granulated sugar
Kosher salt

8 oz. (8 packed cups) baby spinach
8 oz. (4 cups) thinly sliced cremini
    mushrooms
1 cup fresh flat-leaf parsley leaves
1 cup coarsely chopped roasted
    unsalted cashews

Blend the tahini, lemon juice, miso, paprika, sugar, ⅛ tsp. salt, and ¼ cup water in a blender until smooth.

In a large bowl, toss the spinach, mushrooms, parsley, and cashews with the dressing. Serve.

wilted arugula salad with asparagus, bacon, almonds & sherry vinaigrette

SERVES 4

7 oz. (8 strips) bacon, cut crosswise into 2-inch pieces

1 lb. asparagus, trimmed of tough, woody stems and cut crosswise into 1-inch pieces

Kosher salt and freshly ground black pepper

3 Tbs. sherry vinegar

2 Tbs. extra-virgin olive oil

½ tsp. Dijon mustard

6 oz. baby arugula

⅓ cup slivered almonds, toasted

Heat a 12-inch skillet over medium-high heat. Cook the bacon, stirring often, until crisp, 5 minutes. With a slotted spoon, transfer to a paper-towel-lined plate to drain, leaving the bacon fat in the skillet.

Cook the asparagus in the skillet with the bacon fat, stirring often, until crisp-tender and browned in spots, 3 minutes. Season with ¼ tsp. salt and, using a slotted spoon, transfer to the plate with the bacon. Add the vinegar, olive oil, mustard, ½ tsp. salt, and a scant ¼ tsp. pepper to the fat in the skillet and whisk until combined.

In a large bowl, combine the asparagus, bacon, arugula, and almonds and toss with just enough warm vinaigrette to wilt the arugula. Serve immediately.

asparagus salad with orange, prosciutto & pistachios

SERVES 4

1 lb. asparagus, trimmed
¼ cup plus 2 Tbs. extra-virgin olive oil
½ tsp. kosher salt
2 medium oranges
8 thin slices prosciutto

8 Tbs. coarsely chopped roasted shelled pistachios
Freshly ground black pepper
1 oz. Parmigiano-Reggiano, shaved with a vegetable peeler

Transfer the asparagus to a glass loaf pan with ½ cup water, 1 Tbs. olive oil, and the salt. Toss then cover tightly with plastic wrap. Microwave on high until the asparagus is crisp-tender, about 5 minutes.

Meanwhile, with a knife, segment the oranges over a bowl, squeezing the empty membranes to get all the juice; reserve the juice.

Divide the asparagus among four salad plates. Very coarsely tear the prosciutto and arrange over the asparagus. Divide the orange segments among the plates. Top each serving with 2 Tbs. of the pistachios, 1 Tbs. extra-virgin olive oil, 1 Tbs. of the reserved orange juice, and a few grinds of black pepper. Garnish with the Parmigiano and serve.

strawberry and spinach salad with herbs and goat cheese

SERVES 4

3 cups baby spinach
1 cup packed small mixed fresh herb leaves such as basil, mint, and parsley
2 Tbs. packed tarragon leaves
1 cup quartered strawberries

Kosher salt and freshly ground black pepper
3 Tbs. extra-virgin olive oil
1 Tbs. fresh lemon juice
3 oz. fresh goat cheese

In a large salad bowl, combine the spinach, mixed herbs, and tarragon leaves. Gently toss with the strawberries and a few pinches of salt and pepper.

In a small bowl, whisk together the olive oil, lemon juice, ¼ tsp. salt, and ¼ tsp. pepper. Toss the salad with enough vinaigrette to coat and crumble the goat cheese on top.

tip

Feel free to tinker with the proportions of the herbs, but be careful about increasing the amount of the tarragon; it can become overpowering.

pea, butter lettuce & herb salad

SERVES 4

1 cup fresh shelled peas (about 1 lb. unshelled) or frozen peas

Kosher salt and freshly ground black pepper

3 Tbs. extra-virgin olive oil

1 Tbs. fresh lemon juice

1 tsp. finely grated lemon zest

1 small head butter lettuce, washed and dried, leaves torn into bite-size pieces

6 medium radishes, thinly sliced

4 scallions (white and light-green parts), thinly sliced on the diagonal

¼ cup loosely packed fresh flat-leaf parsley leaves

¼ cup loosely packed fresh chervil leaves

2 Tbs. very coarsely chopped fresh tarragon

2 Tbs. thinly sliced chives

3 oz. ricotta salata, shaved thinly with a vegetable peeler (optional)

If using fresh peas, sample them. If they are young, sweet, and tender, keep them raw. If they are older and a bit tough, blanch them in a small pot of boiling salted water until just tender, 2 to 4 minutes. Drain and spread them on a baking sheet in a single layer to cool. If using frozen peas, thaw them by leaving them at room temperature or by running them under warm water.

In a small bowl, whisk the oil with the lemon juice, lemon zest, and salt and pepper to taste.

Just before serving, toss the peas in a small bowl with 1 Tbs. of the dressing. Toss the butter lettuce, radishes, scallions, and herbs in a large bowl with just enough of the remaining dressing to lightly coat. Season to taste with salt and pepper.

Arrange the salad on individual serving plates and top with the peas and the ricotta salata (if using).

tip

This salad is best with very fresh, young peas that are tender enough to be eaten just barely blanched or even raw.

quinoa, cucumber & radish salad with miso vinaigrette

SERVES 6

2¾ cups plus ⅓ cup lower-salt vegetable or chicken broth

3 Tbs. white miso

3 Tbs. seasoned rice vinegar

2 Tbs. soy sauce, preferably reduced sodium

1 Tbs. Asian sesame oil

½ cup canola or other neutral vegetable oil

2 Tbs. chopped sweet pickled sushi ginger

1½ cups quinoa, preferably red, well rinsed

1 medium English cucumber, sliced into ¼-inch-thick half-moons

10 oz. radishes, cut into bite-size pieces (about 2 cups)

2 oz. hearty baby greens, such as arugula or kale, or a mix (about 2 packed cups)

Put ⅓ cup of the broth and the miso, vinegar, soy sauce, and sesame oil in a blender; blend to combine. With the motor running, slowly add the canola oil to make a creamy dressing. Add the ginger and pulse a couple of times to very finely chop. (Alternatively, very finely chop the ginger and whisk the ingredients together.)

In a 2- to 3-quart saucepan, bring the remaining 2¾ cups broth to a simmer over

tip

If you can, buy small radishes in bunches with the greens still attached; these are fresher than those in plastic bags.

medium heat. Add the quinoa, cover, turn the heat down to medium low, and cook until the quinoa is tender and the liquid is absorbed, 10 to 15 minutes. Remove from the heat and let stand for 3 to 5 minutes. Uncover and fluff with a fork. Let cool to room temperature, about 30 minutes.

Toss the quinoa, cucumber, radishes, and greens together. Add ¾ cup of the vinaigrette, toss, and serve, passing the remaining dressing at the table. (Save the remaining vinaigrette for other salads; it will keep for at least 3 days in the refrigerator.)

black rice salad with sugar snap peas and avocado

SERVES 6

10½ oz. (1½ cups) Chinese black rice
3 Tbs. peanut or olive oil
½ cup minced shallots
1 fresh cayenne or serrano chile with seeds, minced (optional)
3 Tbs. fresh lime juice
2 Tbs. seasoned rice vinegar
1 Tbs. Thai fish sauce (preferably Squid® brand)
Kosher salt

4 oz. sugar snap peas, trimmed and sliced ½ inch thick on the diagonal (1 cup)
2 small firm-ripe avocados, halved, pitted, and peeled; 1 cut into ½-inch dice and 1 thinly sliced
¼ cup chopped fresh mint
1 to 2 limes, cut into wedges

Put the rice in a bowl and fill with cold water. Swish the rice with your fingers to release excess starch, then pour off the water. Repeat two or three more times until the water is less cloudy. Drain the rice and transfer to a heavy-duty 3-quart saucepan. Add 2¾ cups water, set over high heat, and bring to a boil. Cover, lower the heat to low, and cook until the rice is tender but intact, about 30 minutes. Remove from the heat and let stand, uncovered, until cooled to room temperature. (The rice can be made up to 2 hours ahead.)

Meanwhile, heat the oil in an 8-inch skillet over medium heat. Add the shallots and cook, stirring often, until translucent, 2 to 3 minutes.

Stir in the chile, if using, and cook, stirring, for 1 minute. Remove from the heat.

Combine the lime juice, rice vinegar, fish sauce, and ½ tsp. salt in a large bowl.

Wet a large wooden spoon with water and use it to turn the rice gently to loosen it. Transfer to the bowl with the dressing, add the shallot mixture, and gently toss to combine. Let the salad sit at room temperature for at least 10 minutes and up to 1 hour to let the flavors blend. Stir in the sugar snap peas, diced avocado, and half of the mint; season to taste with salt. Transfer to a shallow serving dish and garnish with the sliced avocado and the remaining mint. Serve at room temperature with the lime wedges on the side.

lemony orzo soup with baby spinach and peas

SERVES 4

6 cups lower-salt chicken broth
½ cup orzo
1½ tsp. dried oregano
Kosher salt and freshly ground black pepper
¼ cup coarsely grated yellow onion
1½ oz. finely grated Parmigiano-Reggiano or pecorino romano (1½ cups using a rasp grater)
3 oz. (3 packed cups) baby spinach
½ cup frozen peas
2 Tbs. fresh lemon juice

Combine the broth, orzo, oregano, and 1 tsp. salt in a 3- to 4-quart pot. Cover and bring to a boil over high heat. Uncover, add the onion, and reduce the heat to medium. Simmer until the orzo is just tender, 2 to 3 minutes. Remove from the heat, and whisk in the Parmigiano until fully incorporated. Stir in the spinach, peas, and lemon juice. Season to taste with salt and pepper, and serve immediately.

tip

Use vegetable broth instead of chicken broth to make the soup vegetarian.

chilled sorrel, potato & leek soup

SERVES 4 TO 5

1 Tbs. unsalted butter

1 medium leek (white and light-green parts only), thinly sliced (about 1 cup)

Kosher salt and freshly ground black pepper

2 small Yukon Gold potatoes, peeled and cut into small dice (about 2 cups)

1 cup lower-salt chicken broth

4 oz. sorrel leaves, ribs removed; more for garnish

1 Tbs. plain yogurt

Melt the butter in a 4-quart pot over medium-low heat. Add the leek and a pinch of salt and cook until tender but not brown, 5 to 7 minutes. Stir in the potatoes and then add 3 cups of water, the broth, and 1 tsp. salt. Bring to a boil, cover partially, reduce the heat to maintain a simmer, and cook until the potatoes are tender, about 12 minutes. Add the sorrel and cook until wilted, 1 to 2 minutes. Remove from the heat and let cool slightly.

Purée the soup in a blender until smooth. Pour the soup into a medium bowl, cover, and refrigerate until completely chilled, about 4 hours.

Whisk the yogurt into the soup and season to taste with salt and pepper. Serve garnished with thinly sliced or chopped sorrel leaves.

asparagus soup with saffron croutons

SERVES 6 TO 8

For the croutons

3 to 4 slices of fine-grain white
  bread, such as Pepperidge Farm®
2 Tbs. extra-virgin olive oil
¼ tsp. saffron threads
Kosher salt

For the soup

2 bunches asparagus (about 2 lb.)
4 Tbs. unsalted butter

2 large shallots, chopped
  (about ½ cup)
2 cups heavy cream
Kosher salt and freshly ground white
  pepper
½ tsp. fresh lemon juice; more to
  taste
2 tsp. thinly sliced chives

Make the croutons

Cut the crust off the bread and discard. Cut the bread into tiny cubes
(about ⅓ inch) to yield about 1½ cups.

Heat the olive oil in a 10-inch sauté pan over medium-low heat.
Crumble the saffron and gently cook for about 1 minute to infuse the
oil with the saffron color; watch carefully—saffron can burn quickly.
Add the bread cubes and toss to coat with the oil. Sprinkle with ¼ tsp.
salt and cook, stirring occasionally, until the croutons are golden and
crunchy, 3 to 4 minutes. Transfer the croutons to a plate to cool. (Once
completely cooled, they can be stored in an airtight container for a
couple of days.)

Make the soup

Trim the tough bottoms off the asparagus and cut the rest of the spears into 1-inch pieces.

Melt the butter in a 3- to 4-quart saucepan over medium-low heat. Add the shallots, and cook, stirring occasionally, until soft but not colored, about 5 minutes. Add the cream, 2 cups of water, 2 tsp. salt, and ½ tsp. white pepper. Increase the heat to high and bring the liquid to a boil. Add the asparagus, lower to a simmer, and cook until the asparagus is tender (taste a piece to see) but still quite green, about 5 minutes.

Purée the soup in batches in a blender and pass it through a fine-mesh strainer, pressing on the solids, into a bowl (if you plan to serve it cold) or into a clean saucepan. (The soup will keep, covered and refrigerated, for up to 2 days.)

To serve, reheat the soup if serving it warm. Stir in the lemon juice. Season to taste with salt and pepper and more lemon juice, if you like. Serve the soup in cups or small bowls, topped with the croutons and chives.

carrot and leek soup with herbed croutons

SERVES 6

6 Tbs. unsalted butter
1 medium yellow onion, chopped
2 small leeks (light-green and white parts only), sliced
2 large cloves garlic, chopped
Kosher salt and freshly ground black pepper
3 cups lower-salt chicken broth
2 lb. carrots, sliced ¼ inch thick
3 fresh or 2 dried bay leaves
2 sprigs fresh thyme
4 oz. crusty bread, cut into ½-inch cubes (2 cups)
1½ Tbs. chopped fresh chervil
1 cup plain full-fat or low-fat yogurt

Position a rack in the center of the oven and heat the oven to 350°F.

In a 4- to 5-quart saucepan, melt 3 Tbs. of the butter over medium heat. Add the onion, leeks, garlic, ½ tsp. salt, and ¼ tsp. pepper; cook until softened and light golden-brown, about 10 minutes.

Add the broth, carrots, bay leaves, thyme sprigs, and ½ cup water; bring to a boil over medium-high heat. Reduce the heat to medium and simmer until the carrots are tender, about 15 minutes.

tip

If you can't find chervil (a relative of the carrot), use dill instead.

Meanwhile, melt the remaining 3 Tbs. butter in a 3-quart saucepan over medium heat. Add the bread cubes and chopped chervil and toss to coat evenly. Spread on a rimmed baking sheet, season with salt, and bake until golden, 8 to 10 minutes.

When the vegetables are tender, discard the bay leaves and thyme sprigs. With a regular or a hand-held blender, purée the soup (work in batches if using a regular blender). Stir in the yogurt. If you prefer a thinner texture, add a little water. Season to taste with salt and pepper, and serve garnished with the chervil croutons.

pea and parmigiano soup

SERVES 4

3 Tbs. unsalted butter
½ cup finely chopped shallots
¼ cup dry white wine
3 cups lower-salt chicken broth
1 large Yukon Gold potato (8 oz.),
    peeled and cut into ½-inch
    cubes (1 cup)

10 oz. (2 cups) frozen peas
1½ oz. finely grated Parmigiano-
    Reggiano (1½ cups using a rasp
    grater)
Freshly ground black pepper
White truffle oil, for garnish
    (optional)

Melt 2 Tbs. of the butter in a 3-quart saucepan over medium-low heat. Add the shallots and cook, stirring often, until softened, 3 to 5 minutes. Add the wine, raise the heat to medium high, and cook until almost evaporated, about 2 minutes. Add the broth and potato and bring to a boil. Lower the heat to medium low, cover, and cook until the potatoes are tender when poked with a fork, 6 to 8 minutes. Add the peas, cover the pan, and cook until heated through, about 5 minutes more.

Purée the soup in 2 batches in a blender until very smooth.

Reheat the soup in a 2-quart saucepan over medium-low heat. Add the Parmigiano, the remaining 1 Tbs. butter, and ½ tsp. pepper and cook, stirring, until melted. Serve drizzled with the truffle oil, if using. (The soup can be made a day ahead and refrigerated, covered.)

broccoli raab and cannellini beans over garlic bread

SERVES 2

1 bunch broccoli raab, washed

1½ Tbs. extra-virgin olive oil; more for drizzling

1 small onion, finely chopped

1½ to 2 tsp. finely chopped fresh rosemary

2 cloves garlic, minced, plus 1 whole clove to rub on the toast

Dried red chile flakes

One 15-oz. can cannellini beans, rinsed and drained

Kosher salt and freshly ground black pepper to taste

2 to 4 thick slices sturdy country-style bread, preferably sourdough

Lemon wedges or red-wine vinegar

Peel the larger stems of the broccoli raab and slice them thinly. Chop the leaves coarsely. Heat the oil in a 10-inch skillet. Add the onion and rosemary and cook over medium-high heat until the onion softens and begins to color, about 5 minutes. Add the minced garlic and a pinch of chile flakes and cook for 1 minute longer. Add the chopped raab leaves and stems along with 1 cup of water; cook, stirring occasionally, until the raab is wilted, about 5 minutes. Add the beans (and more water as needed) and cook for another 15 minutes. Season with salt and pepper.

Toast the bread on the grill or under the broiler. Rub one side of the toast with the garlic clove. Set a slice or two of toast on each plate. Spoon the beans and greens over top. Drizzle oil liberally over the beans and greens. Top with a squeeze of lemon juice or a splash of vinegar.

indian vegetable curry

SERVES 4 TO 5

1 cup unsweetened coconut milk

12 oz. cauliflower florets, cut into bite-size pieces (about 3 cups)

1 large carrot, sliced ¼ inch thick on the diagonal

1 medium yellow onion, halved and thinly sliced lengthwise

1 Tbs. minced fresh ginger

2 tsp. minced garlic

2 tsp. hot curry powder, such as Madras

Kosher salt

3 oz. baby spinach (about 3 lightly packed cups)

One 15-oz. can chickpeas, drained and rinsed

2 medium plum tomatoes, cut into ½-inch dice

3 Tbs. chopped fresh cilantro

In a 12-inch skillet set over medium-low heat, stir together the coconut milk, cauliflower, carrot, onion, ginger, garlic, curry powder, and 1 tsp. salt. Raise the heat to high and bring to a boil; reduce to a simmer, cover, and cook, stirring often, until the cauliflower is tender when pierced with a knife, about 10 minutes. (If the pan looks dry, stir in water ¼ cup at a time.)

Stir in the spinach, chickpeas, and tomatoes and continue to cook until the chickpeas are heated through and the spinach is wilted, about 5 minutes. Stir in the cilantro, season to taste with salt, and serve.

green goddess scrambled eggs

SERVES 4

1 Tbs. extra-virgin olive oil
6 oz. (6 packed cups) baby spinach
Kosher salt and freshly ground black pepper
8 large eggs

¼ cup thinly sliced fresh chives
1 Tbs. chopped fresh tarragon
Freshly ground black pepper
2 Tbs. unsalted butter
2 Tbs. sour cream

Heat the oil in a 12-inch skillet over medium-high heat. Add the spinach and ½ tsp. salt and cook, tossing occasionally, until the spinach is wilted and any liquid has evaporated, 3 to 4 minutes. Transfer the spinach to a plate, and wipe out the skillet.

Whisk the eggs with the chives, tarragon, ½ tsp. salt, and ⅛ tsp. pepper. Melt the butter in the skillet over medium-high heat. Add the egg mixture and cook, stirring slowly but constantly with a silicone spatula, until the eggs are barely set, 1 to 2 minutes. Add the spinach and gently fold it into the eggs until they are softly set, 1 to 2 minutes. Remove from the heat, gently fold in the sour cream, and serve.

miso-glazed wild salmon with sesame asparagus

SERVES 4 TO 6

½ cup white miso

¼ cup dry sake or dry white wine

¼ cup mirin

1 Tbs. honey

1 Tbs. soy sauce

2 tsp. finely grated fresh ginger

One 1½- to 2-lb. skin-on wild salmon fillet, pin bones removed

1½ lb. medium-thick asparagus, trimmed

2 tsp. vegetable oil; more as needed

½ tsp. kosher salt

1 tsp. Asian sesame oil

1½ tsp. toasted sesame seeds

In a baking dish or on a rimmed baking sheet large enough to accommodate the salmon, whisk the miso, sake, mirin, honey, soy sauce, and ginger until combined. Turn the salmon in the mixture to coat and leave flesh side down. Marinate for 30 minutes at room temperature, or cover and refrigerate for up to 12 hours.

Position a rack 6 inches from the broiler element and heat the broiler on high. In a large bowl, toss the asparagus with the vegetable oil. Line a large rimmed baking sheet with foil and lightly brush with oil. Leaving a light coating of the marinade on the salmon, transfer it skin side down to one side of the sheet. Arrange the asparagus on the other side of the sheet. Sprinkle the salt over the fish and asparagus.

Broil until the salmon is browned around the edges, 2 to 4 minutes. Toss the asparagus and continue to broil until the asparagus is tender and the salmon is cooked to your liking, 3 to 5 minutes more for medium rare and 5 to 7 minutes more for medium. Use a paring knife to check for doneness; medium-rare salmon will be slightly translucent in the center, and medium salmon will be opaque but juicy.

Transfer the salmon and asparagus to a serving platter. Drizzle the sesame oil over the asparagus, sprinkle the sesame seeds over both, and serve.

tip

Make sure the pin bones—small, flexible, needlelike bones—have been removed from the salmon before cooking. To check, run your fingers lengthwise in both directions down the center of the fillet, feeling for the bones. If you find any, use clean needlenose pliers or tweezers to grab the tip of each bone and give it a gentle tug, pulling it out in the same direction it lies.

asparagus, goat cheese & bacon tart

SERVES 4

5 slices bacon
1 shallot, finely chopped
1 bunch asparagus (about 1 lb.), tough ends trimmed, cut into 1-inch pieces
2 Tbs. unbleached all-purpose flour
½ lb. puff pastry, defrosted if frozen
½ lb. soft fresh goat cheese
Kosher salt and freshly ground black pepper
1 large egg yolk mixed with ½ tsp. water

Position a rack in the center of the oven and heat the oven to 450°F.

In a medium frying pan, cook the bacon over medium heat until crisp, about 8 minutes. Transfer to paper towels. Pour off all but 1 Tbs. of the bacon fat from the pan. Add the shallot to the pan and sauté for about 1 minute. Add the asparagus and cook over medium-high heat until the asparagus is crisp-tender, about 5 minutes. Remove the pan from the heat. Crumble the bacon into tiny pieces and mix it with the asparagus and shallot.

tip

To make this tart meatless, simply omit the bacon.

On a lightly floured piece of kitchen parchment, roll out the pastry to a 10x16-inch rectangle. Transfer the pastry and the parchment to a baking sheet.

Using your fingers, pat the goat cheese onto the pastry, spreading it as evenly as you can and leaving a 1-inch border around the edge. Sprinkle the asparagus, bacon, and shallot mixture evenly over the goat cheese. Season with salt and pepper.

Brush the edge of the tart with the egg wash. Bake until the pastry is golden-brown, 20 to 25 minutes. Let cool slightly and serve warm.

spinach and white bean salad with tuna

SERVES 4

2 Tbs. brine-packed capers, rinsed and drained
1 medium clove garlic
Kosher salt and freshly ground black pepper
3 Tbs. fresh lemon juice
1 Tbs. Dijon mustard
3 Tbs. extra-virgin olive oil

Two 5-oz. cans albacore tuna, drained
One 15-oz. can cannellini or navy beans, rinsed and drained
½ small red onion, very thinly sliced
6 oz. (6 packed cups) baby spinach
2 heads red or white Belgian endive, coarsely chopped

Using a chef's knife, mince and mash the capers and garlic with 1 tsp. salt and ¼ tsp. pepper. Scrape into a large bowl and whisk in the lemon juice and mustard. In a slow stream, whisk in the oil until emulsified. Add the tuna, flaking it into large pieces, then the beans, onion, spinach, and endive. Toss gently with the dressing and serve.

tip

Water-packed canned tuna works fine, but choose oil-packed tuna for a richer, more satisfying flavor.

fusilli with peas and feta

SERVES 4

Kosher salt and freshly ground black
  pepper
1½ cups lower-salt chicken broth
1 lb. fresh or frozen peas
  (about 3 cups)
3 Tbs. extra-virgin olive oil

2 Tbs. chopped fresh dill
12 oz. dried fusilli pasta
4 oz. feta, finely crumbled
  (about 1 cup)
Lemon wedges, for serving

Bring a large pot of well-salted water to a boil over
high heat.

In a 3-quart saucepan, bring the chicken
broth to a boil over high heat. Add the peas and
cook until crisp-tender, 2 to 4 minutes. Remove
from the heat and, using a slotted spoon, remove
and reserve 1 cup of the peas. Transfer the broth
and the remaining peas to a blender. Add the
olive oil, all but 1 tsp. of the dill, 1¼ tsp. salt, and
½ tsp. pepper and blend until smooth. It's fine if
the sauce looks thin at this point.

Meanwhile, cook the pasta in the pot of salted
water until al dente. Drain and transfer to a large
bowl. Toss the pasta with the sauce, the reserved
peas, and ¾ cup of the feta. Serve garnished with
the remaining ¼ cup feta and 1 tsp. dill, with lemon
wedges on the side.

tip

If using peas
in the pod,
you'll need about
3 lb. before shelling.

broiled lamb skewers with baby arugula and lemon vinaigrette

SERVES 2

2 Tbs. fresh lemon juice
2 tsp. sour cream
1 small clove garlic, minced
Kosher salt and coarsely ground
   black pepper
¼ cup plus 1 Tbs. extra-virgin olive oil
¾ lb. boneless lamb shoulder chops
   or lamb leg steaks, trimmed of
   extra fat and cut into 1-inch cubes
   (1½ cups)

4 oz. baby arugula (about 4 cups)
½ cup very thinly sliced red onion
   (½ small)
¼ cup crumbled feta or blue cheese
   (1 oz.)

Position an oven rack 4 inches from the broiler element and heat the broiler to high. In a small bowl, combine the lemon juice, sour cream, garlic, and a pinch of salt. Slowly whisk in the ¼ cup olive oil.

In a medium bowl, combine the lamb with the 1 Tbs. olive oil, ½ tsp. salt, and ¼ tsp. pepper. Toss to coat evenly. Thread the lamb onto four small (8-inch) bamboo or metal skewers.

tip

✖ If using bamboo skewers, soak them in water for 30 minutes before threading them.

Put the skewers on a broiler pan and broil the lamb, flipping once, until browned on the outside but still pink inside (medium doneness), 2 to 4 minutes per side. Transfer the skewers to a small, shallow baking dish. Whisk the vinaigrette to recombine and pour 3 Tbs. over the skewers, turning to coat.

In a medium bowl, toss the arugula and onion with enough of the remaining vinaigrette to lightly coat (you may not need it all). Season with salt and pepper to taste. Pile the greens on two plates, top each salad with two lamb skewers, sprinkle with the cheese, and serve immediately.

fettuccine primavera

SERVES 6

Kosher salt and freshly ground black pepper

1 lb. fettuccine

2 Tbs. unsalted butter, cut into chunks

2 cloves garlic, minced

3 cups very thinly sliced mixed spring vegetables, such as asparagus (leave tips whole), baby carrots, baby leeks, baby turnips, baby zucchini, spring onions, and sugar snap peas

1 cup whole, shelled fresh or thawed frozen peas, baby lima beans (preferably peeled), or fava beans (peeled), or a mix of all

1 cup heavy cream

1 Tbs. thinly sliced lemon zest (remove zest with a vegetable peeler and thinly slice)

2 cups loosely packed pea shoots, watercress sprigs, or baby arugula

½ cup freshly grated Parmigiano-Reggiano

½ cup roughly chopped mixed fresh herbs such as basil, chervil, chives, mint, flat-leaf parsley, and tarragon

¼ tsp. crushed red pepper flakes

¼ cup toasted pine nuts

Bring a large pot of generously salted water to a boil and cook the fettuccine, stirring occasionally, until al dente, about 6 minutes. (While the pasta is cooking, scoop 1½ cup of pasta cooking water.)

Meanwhile, melt the butter in a 10-inch straight-sided sauté pan over medium heat. Add the garlic and cook until softened and fragrant but not browned, about 1 minute. Add 1 cup of the reserved pasta water. Add the sliced vegetables and peas or lima beans (if using fresh). Cover and simmer until the vegetables are just tender, about 3 minutes.

Add the cream and lemon zest along with any fava beans or thawed, frozen peas or lima beans (if using). Bring to a simmer.

Drain the fettuccine and return it to its cooking pot. Toss with the vegetables and cream sauce, pea shoots (or watercress or arugula), Parmigiano, all but 1 Tbs. of the herbs, and the pepper flakes. Season to taste with salt and pepper. If necessary, adjust the consistency of the sauce with the reserved ½ cup pasta water; the sauce should generously coat the vegetables and pasta. Serve immediately, sprinkled with the remaining fresh herbs and the pine nuts.

campanelle with broccoli raab, sausage & olives

SERVES 3 TO 4

Kosher salt

1 lb. broccoli raab, thick stems trimmed off, leaves and florets rinsed well

6 oz. dried campanelle pasta (2 cups)

3 Tbs. extra-virgin olive oil

¾ lb. sweet Italian sausage (bulk sausage or links removed from casing)

3 cloves garlic, minced

¼ tsp. crushed red pepper flakes

¾ cup homemade or lower-salt chicken broth

½ cup pitted Kalamata olives, quartered

2 tsp. finely grated lightly packed lemon zest

⅓ cup freshly grated pecorino romano

Bring a large pot of well-salted water to a boil over high heat. Have a bowl of ice water ready. Add the broccoli raab and cook until bright green and tender, 2 minutes (the water doesn't have to come back to a full boil once the broccoli raab has been added). With tongs or a slotted spoon, transfer the broccoli raab to the bowl of ice water to stop the cooking. Drain well and gently squeeze the broccoli raab to remove excess water.

Return the pot of water to a boil, add the pasta, cook according to the package directions, and drain.

While the campanelle cooks, heat the oil in a 12-inch skillet over medium-high heat. Add the sausage and cook, stirring and breaking it into smaller pieces with a wooden spoon, until it's browned and almost cooked through, 4 to 6 minutes. Add the garlic and red pepper flakes and cook until the garlic is lightly golden, about 1 minute. Pour in the broth and bring to a boil; cook, scraping the pan with a wooden spoon occasionally, until the broth is reduced by about half, 3 to 4 minutes. Add the broccoli raab, olives, and lemon zest and cook, stirring, until hot, 1 to 2 minutes. Add the pasta and cheese to the skillet and toss well. Season to taste with salt and serve immediately.

tip

�֎ Blanching the broccoli raab in salted boiling water for a couple of minutes will cut some of its bitterness.

creamy spinach and leeks with seared scallops

SERVES 4

2½ Tbs. unsalted butter

12 oz. baby spinach (about 12 loosely packed cups)

2 medium leeks (white and light-green parts only), halved lengthwise, thinly sliced crosswise, and rinsed (about 1 cup)

Kosher salt and freshly ground black pepper

2 large cloves garlic, minced

⅓ cup dry white wine

⅓ cup heavy cream

Pinch freshly grated nutmeg

2 Tbs. freshly grated Parmigiano-Reggiano

16 large dry-packed sea scallops

4 tsp. vegetable oil

Melt ½ Tbs. of the butter in a 12-inch skillet over medium-high heat. Add half of the spinach and cook, tossing with tongs, until just wilted, about 2 minutes. Transfer with tongs to a colander set over a bowl; let drain and cool slightly. Repeat with the remaining spinach (you don't need to add more butter). Squeeze handfuls of the spinach to release as much liquid as possible.

Discard any liquid in the skillet. Melt the remaining 2 Tbs. butter over medium heat and then add the leeks and a pinch of salt. Cook until softened but not browned, about 5 minutes. Add the garlic and cook, stirring, for 1 minute more. Add the wine, raise the heat to medium high, and cook until almost evaporated, about 2 minutes. Add the cream and simmer until it's thickened and coats the back of a spoon, about

2 minutes. Season with ½ tsp. salt, a generous grind of pepper, and the nutmeg. Stir in the cheese and gently fold in the spinach. Keep warm.

   Pat the scallops dry and remove the side muscle if still attached. In a 12-inch nonstick skillet, heat 2 tsp. of the oil over medium heat until shimmering hot. Season the scallops with salt and pepper. Add half of the scallops to the pan and cook, undisturbed, until browned on the bottom, 2 to 3 minutes. Flip and continue to cook until just opaque in the center, about 2 minutes more. Transfer to a plate and tent with foil to keep warm. Repeat with the remaining 2 tsp. of oil and the scallops. Serve the scallops over the spinach.

honey-mustard turkey cutlets with arugula, carrot & celery salad

SERVES 4

¼ cup unbleached all-purpose flour
Kosher salt and freshly ground black
  pepper
4 Tbs. extra-virgin olive oil
¼ cup whole-grain mustard
1 Tbs. honey
3 Tbs. fresh lemon juice
1 Tbs. finely chopped fresh tarragon
Four 6-oz. turkey cutlets, pounded
  to ⅛ inch thick

2 Tbs. canola oil; more as needed
¼ tsp. ground cumin
2 oz. baby arugula (2 packed cups)
2 medium ribs celery, trimmed and
  sliced ⅛ inch thick on the diagonal
1 medium carrot, thinly shaved with
  a vegetable peeler

Combine the flour, ½ tsp. salt, and ¼ tsp. pepper in a shallow bowl. In another shallow bowl, whisk 2 Tbs. of the olive oil, the mustard, honey, 2 Tbs. of the lemon juice, and 2 tsp. of the tarragon.

Dredge each turkey cutlet in the flour mixture and then the mustard mixture. Transfer to a baking sheet or tray lined with parchment or wax paper.

Heat 1 Tbs. of the canola oil in a 12-inch nonstick skillet over medium heat until shimmering hot. Add two cutlets and cook, flipping once, until golden-brown and just cooked through, 5 to 6 minutes total. Transfer to a clean plate and tent with foil to keep warm. Wipe out the skillet and repeat with the remaining 1 Tbs. canola oil and the remaining cutlets.

Whisk the remaining 2 Tbs. olive oil, 1 Tbs. lemon juice, cumin, ¼ tsp. salt, and ⅛ tsp. pepper in a small bowl. In a large bowl, combine the arugula, celery, and carrots; toss with enough of the dressing to lightly coat. Serve the cutlets topped with the salad, sprinkled with the remaining tarragon, and drizzled with any remaining dressing.

tip

✥ The tarragon is the secret ingredient in the honey-mustard coating. It adds licorice notes that elevate the turkey cutlets without overwhelming them.

pork stir-fry with baby bok choy and cashews

SERVES 4

1 lb. pork tenderloin, trimmed
2 Tbs. soy sauce
1 Tbs. mirin
1 tsp. packed dark brown sugar
1 tsp. cornstarch
Freshly ground white pepper
4 tsp. canola oil
4 medium cloves garlic, minced

2 Tbs. minced fresh ginger (from a 4½-inch piece)
1 lb. baby bok choy (3 to 4 heads), stalks cut crosswise into ½-inch-thick slices, leaves kept separate
¾ cup salted cashews
2 tsp. Asian sesame oil

Slice the tenderloin crosswise into ½-inch-thick medallions. Cut the medallions into ½-inch-thick strips.

In a medium bowl, whisk the soy sauce, mirin, brown sugar, cornstarch, and ¼ tsp. white pepper until the cornstarch and sugar are dissolved. Add the pork, toss to coat, and marinate for 5 to 10 minutes.

Heat 2 tsp. of the canola oil in a 14-inch wok or a 12-inch skillet over high heat until shimmering hot and swirl to coat the pan. Add

tip

A stir-fry is always quick, but to save even more time, prepare the vegetables while the pork marinates. Serve with rice, if you like.

the garlic and ginger and stir-fry until fragrant, about 10 seconds. Add the pork in a single layer and cook, undisturbed, for 1 minute. Turn the heat down to medium high and stir-fry until the meat is nearly cooked through, 2 minutes. Transfer to a serving bowl.

Heat the remaining 2 tsp. canola oil in the wok over medium-high heat. Add the bok choy stalks and stir-fry until crisp-tender, about 2 minutes. Add the pork, bok choy leaves, and cashews, and stir-fry until the leaves are wilted, about 1 minute. Remove from the heat, toss with the sesame oil, and serve.

udon with tofu and stir-fried vegetables

SERVES 4

Kosher salt
¾ lb. dried udon noodles
3 cups lower-salt chicken broth
1 Tbs. plus 2 tsp. oyster sauce
1 Tbs. plus 2 tsp. rice vinegar
4 tsp. Asian sesame oil
¼ cup minced fresh ginger
2 Tbs. canola oil
¾ lb. bok choy, cut crosswise into ¾-inch pieces (4 cups)
3½ oz. shiitake mushrooms, stemmed and thinly sliced (1½ cups)
½ lb. extra-firm tofu, cut into ½-inch cubes
2 medium carrots, cut into matchsticks
3 medium scallions, trimmed and thinly sliced, for garnish

Bring a medium pot of well-salted water to a boil. Add the noodles and cook, stirring, until tender, about 8 minutes. Transfer to a colander and run under cold water to cool slightly. Drain well.

In a medium bowl, mix the chicken broth, oyster sauce, vinegar, and 2 tsp. of the sesame oil.

Heat the ginger and canola oil in a large skillet over medium-high heat until the ginger sizzles steadily for about 30 seconds. Add the bok choy and mushrooms, sprinkle with the remaining 2 tsp. sesame oil and ¾ tsp. salt, and cook, tossing after

tip

Wheat-based Japanese udon noodles are available dried and fresh; dried are flatter and closer in texture to linguine.

1 minute, until the bok choy turns dark green and begins to soften, 3 to 5 minutes. Add the chicken broth mixture, tofu, and carrots and bring to a boil. Reduce to a simmer, cover, and cook until the carrots are soft and the tofu is heated through, 5 to 7 minutes.

Distribute the noodles among four bowls. Spoon the vegetables, tofu, and broth over the noodles. Sprinkle with the scallions and serve.

spaghetti with green garlic and olive oil

SERVES 2

Kosher salt and freshly ground black
   pepper
2 Tbs. extra-virgin olive oil
2 oz. green garlic, green parts cut
   into 3-inch julienne strands, white
   parts thinly sliced

6 oz. thin spaghetti
2 Tbs. freshly grated Parmigiano-
   Reggiano; more for serving

Bring 3 quarts of well-salted water to a boil in a large pot over high heat.

Meanwhile, heat the oil in a 10-inch straight-sided sauté pan over low heat. Add the green garlic and 2 big pinches of salt; stir to coat. Cover and cook, stirring frequently, until wilted and softened, 5 to 7 minutes. Remove the pan from the heat.

Boil the spaghetti in the pot of salted water until just al dente, about 1 minute less than the package timing. Set aside about ½ cup of the cooking water and drain the pasta.

Return the sauté pan to low heat. Add the spaghetti and ¼ cup of the cooking water; toss well. Add the Parmigiano and 2 Tbs. of the water; toss again. Season to taste with salt and pepper, adding the remaining water if the pasta seems dry.

Serve in pasta bowls, sprinkled with additional Parmigiano.

fresh mozzarella and spinach pesto melts

SERVES 4

4 oz. (4 packed cups) baby spinach

1 oz. finely grated Parmigiano-Reggiano (1 cup using a rasp grater)

¼ cup pine nuts

1 Tbs. fresh lemon juice

Kosher salt and freshly ground black pepper

2 Tbs. extra-virgin olive oil

4 large slices of rustic white bread

1 large garlic clove, cut in half crosswise

8 oz. fresh mozzarella, thinly sliced

½ cup pitted, chopped Kalamata olives

Position a rack 8 inches from the broiler, place a baking sheet on it, and heat the broiler.

Pulse the spinach, Parmigiano, pine nuts, lemon juice, ½ tsp. salt, and ¼ tsp. pepper in a food processor until chopped. With the motor running, drizzle in the oil to make a smooth, creamy pesto.

Put the bread on the hot baking sheet and toast until the tops are golden. Rub the toasted sides with one garlic clove half, then spread each with about 2 Tbs. of the pesto. (Save the remaining pesto for another use.) Arrange the mozzarella over the pesto. Top with the olives. Broil just until the cheese is melted, 2 to 5 minutes. Serve immediately.

grilled chicken and strawberries with balsamic syrup

SERVES 4

3 Tbs. balsamic vinegar
20 medium strawberries (unhulled)
Four 5-oz. boneless, skinless chicken
    breast cutlets
Extra-virgin olive oil

Kosher salt and freshly ground
    black pepper
2 Tbs. chopped fresh basil

In a 1-quart saucepan, boil the vinegar until reduced by half, about 2 minutes; set aside.

Thread 5 strawberries on each of 4 skewers. Brush the chicken cutlets with olive oil and season with salt and pepper. Heat a grill or grill pan over medium-high heat.

Grill the chicken and strawberries until the chicken is cooked through, 2 to 3 minutes per side, and the strawberries have slight grill marks, 1 to 2 minutes per side. Serve drizzled with a little olive oil and the reduced vinegar and sprinkled with basil.

tip

Grilling gives strawberries a slightly smoky flavor and a striking appearance.

thai-style stir-fried chicken and basil

SERVES 2 TO 3

2 Tbs. vegetable oil
4 medium shallots, peeled and thinly sliced
2 medium cloves garlic, thinly sliced
¼ tsp. crushed red pepper flakes
1 lb. chicken breast cutlets (about ¼ inch thick), cut crosswise into 1-inch-wide strips

1 Tbs. fish sauce
1 Tbs. fresh lime juice
2 tsp. packed light brown sugar
1 cup lightly packed fresh basil leaves

Heat the oil in a well-seasoned wok or a heavy-duty 12-inch skillet over medium-high heat until shimmering hot. Add the shallots, garlic, and red pepper flakes; cook, stirring frequently, until the shallots start to soften but not brown, 1 to 2 minutes. Add the chicken and cook, stirring, until it's no longer pink and the shallots are beginning to brown, 2 to 3 minutes.

Add the fish sauce, lime juice, sugar, and ¼ cup water. Cook, stirring frequently, until the chicken is just cooked through and the liquid reduces to a saucy consistency, 2 to 3 minutes. (If the sauce reduces before the chicken is cooked through, add water, 1 Tbs. at a time.) Remove from the heat, add the basil, and stir to wilt it.

roasted asparagus and fresh herb grilled cheese

SERVES 2

8 thick asparagus spears, tough ends trimmed

2 Tbs. extra-virgin olive oil; more for the bread

Kosher salt and coarsely ground black pepper

4 oz. coarsely grated mozzarella (about 1¼ cups)

1 oz. coarsely grated Parmigiano-Reggiano (about ¼ cup)

2 Tbs. whole-milk ricotta

1 Tbs. finely chopped fresh flat-leaf parsley

1½ tsp. finely chopped fresh mint

1½ tsp. finely chopped fresh basil

½ tsp. finely chopped rinsed capers

1 small clove garlic, minced

¼ tsp. fresh lemon juice

Four ½-inch-thick slices olive bread, preferably from a boule

Position an oven rack in the center of the oven and heat the oven to 400°F.

Cut the asparagus on a sharp angle into 2-inch pieces (if very thick, halve lengthwise first). Toss with 1 Tbs. of the oil on a small rimmed baking sheet. Season with salt and pepper and roast until tender, 7 to 9 minutes. Set aside to cool.

In a small bowl, combine the cheeses and a pinch of pepper. In another small bowl, toss the herbs with the capers, the remaining 1 Tbs. oil, the garlic, lemon juice, and a pinch of salt.

Divide the cheese mixture evenly among the 4 slices of bread. Top 2 slices with the asparagus and then the herb-garlic mixture. Top with the other slices of bread to make 2 sandwiches.

Heat a griddle or 12-inch heavy-duty skillet over medium-low heat. Brush one side of each sandwich with olive oil, put in the pan oiled side down, and then brush the other side with oil. Cook, pressing lightly on the sandwiches with a spatula, until golden-brown on one side, 2 to 3 minutes. Flip and cook until the cheese has melted and the other side is golden-brown, another 2 to 3 minutes. Allow the sandwiches to sit for about 1 minute before slicing in half and serving.

asparagus and fried eggs on garlic toast

SERVES 4

Four ½-inch-thick slices sourdough bread (from a round loaf)
1 large clove garlic, halved
1 Tbs. extra-virgin olive oil; more for brushing the toast
1 lb. asparagus, trimmed of tough, woody stems

Kosher salt and freshly ground black pepper
4 large eggs
1 oz. pecorino romano, shaved into large shards with a vegetable peeler

Lightly toast the bread. Rub one side of each slice with the garlic and brush lightly with olive oil. Put 1 slice on each of four plates.

Put the asparagus in a 12-inch nonstick skillet with ½ cup water, the 1 Tbs. olive oil, and ½ tsp. salt. Cover, bring to a boil over medium-high heat, and cook until tender, about 5 minutes.

Meanwhile, crack the eggs into a shallow bowl. When the asparagus is ready, pat dry and divide it among the pieces of toast. Wipe out the skillet with paper towels if wet; then slide the eggs into the hot skillet, sprinkle each with a pinch of salt and pepper, cover, and cook over low heat until the whites are firm but the yolks are still runny, about 2 minutes.

Top each toast with an egg. Garnish with the shaved pecorino and serve.

toasted israeli couscous salad with mint, cucumber & feta

SERVES 4 TO 6

Kosher salt and freshly ground
   black pepper
1 cup Israeli couscous
1 medium English cucumber, peeled
   and finely diced (2 cups)
½ cup coarsely chopped fresh
   spearmint or pineapple mint
   leaves; additional sprigs for garnish

¼ cup extra-virgin olive oil
2 Tbs. fresh lemon juice; more as
   needed
1 tsp. finely grated lemon zest
1 cup small-diced feta cheese

In a large saucepan, bring 2 quarts well-salted water to a boil.

Meanwhile, in a medium skillet over medium heat, toast the couscous, stirring frequently, until golden-brown, about 7 minutes.

Cook the couscous in the boiling water until tender, about 10 minutes. Drain and rinse under cold running water until cool. Pour the couscous into a large mixing bowl. Stir in the cucumber and mint.

In a small bowl, mix the oil, lemon juice and zest, ¾ tsp. salt, and ¼ tsp. pepper. Stir in the feta. Add the feta mixture to the couscous, season to taste with salt, pepper, and lemon juice, and mix well. Transfer to a serving bowl and garnish with the mint sprigs.

fennel slaw with grapefruit, cracked pepper & pistachios

SERVES 4

3 Tbs. extra-virgin olive oil; more for drizzling

1½ Tbs. white-wine vinegar

2 large fennel bulbs with fronds (about 3 lb.), trimmed (reserve fronds), halved lengthwise, cored, and very thinly sliced

⅓ cup shelled unsalted pistachios, lightly toasted and coarsely chopped

Flaky sea salt, such as Maldon, and coarsely cracked black pepper

1 large pink grapefruit

In a large bowl, whisk the oil and vinegar. Add the fennel and half of the nuts. Finely chop the reserved fronds and add half of them to the bowl. Crumble ½ tsp. salt into the bowl, add a generous pinch of cracked pepper, and toss to coat.

Slice off the ends of the grapefruit to expose the fruit. Stand the fruit on a cut end, and slice off the skin and pith, following the natural curve of the fruit from top to bottom. Cut on each side of each membrane to free the segments, then cut the segments in half and add them to the fennel. Toss gently and season to taste with salt. Serve immediately topped with the remaining fronds and nuts, a pinch of pepper, and a light drizzle of oil.

korean pickled radish

YIELDS 1¼ CUPS; SERVES 6

One 5-oz. piece daikon (3 to 4 inches
  long), peeled
1 Tbs. granulated sugar
1½ tsp. plain rice vinegar
1 tsp. gochugaru (Korean red chile
  flakes) or crushed red pepper
  flakes, or to taste

¼ tsp. minced garlic
½ tsp. kosher salt

Using a mandoline or a sharp chef's knife, cut
the daikon lengthwise into ⅛-inch strips. Transfer
to a large bowl and gently mix in the remaining
ingredients. Cover and refrigerate until chilled,
at least 1 hour. Drain the excess liquid and
serve cold.

tip

✧ The dish can
be made up to
2 days ahead. Drain
just before serving.

fava beans with prosciutto, mint & garlic

SERVES 2

2 Tbs. extra-virgin olive oil
2 Tbs. minced prosciutto
1 tsp. minced garlic
1½ lb. fresh fava beans in the pod,
    shelled, parboiled, and peeled to
    yield 1 scant cup
½ tsp. coarse salt; more to taste

½ tsp. balsamic vinegar
8 large mint leaves, finely chopped
    (to yield 2 to 3 tsp.)

In a medium skillet, heat the olive oil over medium heat. Add the prosciutto and sauté for 1 minute. Add the garlic and sauté, stirring constantly, until it's very fragrant and just beginning to turn brown, another 1 to 2 minutes. Add the fava beans, season with the salt, and sauté until the favas are heated and coated well with the pan contents, another 2 minutes. (Some of the beans will begin to turn a lighter color.) Add the balsamic, turn off the heat, and stir to coat. Add the mint and stir to combine and wilt it. Taste for salt; depending on the saltiness of your prosciutto, you might want to add more.

tip

✕ Fava beans have two protective layers: a pod with a soft, furry lining and a tough skin around each bean. Popping the beans out of the pod is easy— parboil the beans to loosen the skin around the bean just enough for you to pinch it off.

sautéed asparagus with butter and parmesan

SERVES 6 TO 8

1½ lb. asparagus, trimmed
3 Tbs. unsalted butter
½ tsp. kosher salt
¼ tsp. freshly ground black pepper

1 Tbs. minced fresh flat-leaf parsley
¼ cup freshly grated Parmigiano-
   Reggiano

Slice the asparagus on a sharp diagonal about ½ inch thick, leaving the tips whole. Melt the butter in a large (12-inch) skillet over moderate heat. Add the asparagus and season with the salt and pepper. Cook, stirring often, until the asparagus is just tender, 5 to 6 minutes, lowering the heat if needed to keep the asparagus from browning. Don't overcook; the asparagus will soften a little more as it cools.

Remove the pan from the heat. Stir in the parsley and 3 tablespoons of the cheese. Transfer to a serving bowl, top with the remaining cheese, and serve immediately.

tip

✖ You can embellish this dish by adding peas or fava beans to make a spring vegetable mélange, or toss the sautéed asparagus with hot pasta for a main course.

sautéed spinach with golden raisins, pine nuts & breadcrumbs

SERVES 4

¼ cup golden raisins
¼ cup pine nuts, toasted
¼ cup extra-virgin olive oil
½ cup fresh coarse breadcrumbs

1 large clove garlic, minced
Kosher salt
1 bunch fresh spinach (about 1 lb.), trimmed

In a large (12-inch) skillet over medium heat, heat the raisins and pine nuts in 2 Tbs. of the oil for about 1 minute. With a slotted spoon, transfer the raisins and pine nuts to a plate. Add the breadcrumbs and garlic to the pan, and sprinkle with ¼ tsp. salt. Cook over medium-low heat until slightly brown, 5 to 7 minutes. Transfer to a plate.

Put the remaining 2 Tbs. oil in the pan with the spinach and cook until the spinach just wilts. Transfer to a serving platter, toss with the raisins and pine nuts, top with breadcrumbs, and serve.

tip

Making fresh breadcrumbs is simple. Use stale bread or toast fresh bread in a 300°F oven for a few minutes until crisp, then pulse in a food processor until the bread is the size of peas.

glazed carrots with tarragon

SERVES 4

1 lb. carrots, cut into ½-inch rounds
   (about 2 ½ cups)
3 Tbs. unsalted butter
1½ tsp. granulated sugar

Kosher salt
2 Tbs. finely chopped fresh
   tarragon

Put the carrots in an 8-inch-wide, 3- to 4-quart saucepan and arrange snugly. Add the butter, sugar, ½ tsp. salt, and enough water to just cover the carrots (about 2 cups). Bring to a boil over high heat.

Cook over high heat, shaking the pan occasionally, until the liquid has reduced to a syrupy glaze and the carrots are tender, about 10 minutes. (If the glaze is done before the carrots, add about ½ cup water and continue to cook. If the carrots are done first, remove them and continue to boil the liquid until syrupy.)

Lower the heat to medium low, add the tarragon, and toss to combine. Season to taste with salt and serve. (The glazed carrots can be kept warm, covered, for about 20 minutes.)

pea, morel & fiddlehead ragout

SERVES 4

Kosher salt and freshly ground black
  pepper
1 cup fresh or frozen peas
2 Tbs. extra-virgin olive oil
4 oz. fresh morel mushrooms,
  cleaned, trimmed, and thickly
  sliced
4 oz. fiddlehead ferns, washed and
  trimmed

2 cups baby spinach
½ cup vegetable or chicken broth
4 Tbs. unsalted butter
1 Tbs. chopped fresh flat-leaf
  parsley
1 Tbs. chopped fresh chives

Bring a small pot of lightly salted water to a boil over high heat. Have a
bowl of ice water ready. Cook the peas until bright green and tender,
about 30 seconds for fresh and 1 to 2 minutes for frozen. Quickly
transfer the peas to the bowl of ice water. When completely cool, drain
the peas and set aside.

In a large (12-inch) skillet, heat the olive oil over medium-high heat.
Add the morels and fiddleheads and let them brown well on one side,
about 2 minutes. Add the peas, spinach, broth, butter, and a pinch of
salt. Cook, stirring occasionally, until the spinach wilts and the liquid
reduces to a glaze, about 5 minutes. Add the parsley and chives and
season to taste with salt and pepper. Serve immediately.

radish, carrot & edamame stir-fry

SERVES 4 TO 6

5 medium carrots (about ¾ lb.), peeled
1¾ lb. radishes (about 2 bunches), trimmed
2 Tbs. mirin
1 Tbs. reduced-sodium soy sauce
½ tsp. kosher salt

1 Tbs. peanut oil
1 Tbs. minced garlic
1 Tbs. minced fresh ginger
⅔ cup shelled edamame (fresh or frozen)
1 tsp. sesame seeds, toasted

Halve each carrot lengthwise, then cut each half on the diagonal into ¼-inch-thick slices. Slice the radishes crosswise into ¼-inch-thick rounds.

In a small bowl, combine the mirin, soy sauce, and salt.

Heat a 14-inch flat-bottom wok (or a 12-inch heavy-duty skillet) over high heat. Swirl in the oil. Add the carrots and radishes and cook, stirring often, until the edges begin to brown, 5 to 7 minutes. Add the garlic and ginger and continue to cook, stirring constantly, until the vegetables are crisp-tender, about 2 minutes more. Add the edamame (thawed, if using frozen) and the soy sauce mixture and cook, stirring, until just heated through, about 1 minute. Stir in the sesame seeds and serve.

japanese spinach with sesame and soy

SERVES 4

Kosher salt
1 lb. baby spinach (about 16 loosely
  packed cups)
2 Tbs. plus 1 tsp. toasted sesame
  seeds

1 tsp. granulated sugar
4½ tsp. soy sauce
1 Tbs. unseasoned rice vinegar
½ tsp. Asian sesame oil

Bring an 8-quart pot of salted water to a boil. Fill a medium bowl with ice water. Add the spinach to the pot, pressing it into the water with a slotted spoon, and cook for 20 seconds. Remove with the spoon and plunge into the ice water. Transfer the spinach to a colander, spreading it out to drain. Using a clean, folded dishtowel, press down on the spinach to remove as much water as possible. Toss the spinach, spread it out, and press it again if necessary, using a fresh towel. Line a baking sheet with paper towels, spread the spinach on top, cover with paper towels, and chill for 30 minutes.

Using a spice grinder, grind 2 Tbs. of the sesame seeds with ½ tsp. of the sugar. In a medium bowl, combine the remaining ½ tsp. sugar with the soy sauce, vinegar, and sesame oil. Stir in the ground sesame seeds.

Add the chilled spinach and gently toss it with your hands, separating any clumps. Serve sprinkled with the remaining sesame seeds.

sautéed chayote with sweet onion and bacon

SERVES 4

3 slices bacon (about 2 oz.), cut into
  ½-inch pieces
1½ lb. chayote (about 2 large),
  peeled, quartered lengthwise,
  seeded, and sliced crosswise
  ¼ inch thick
1 medium sweet onion (about 8 oz.),
  thinly sliced into half-moons

3 medium cloves garlic, pressed or
  minced
2 Tbs. dry white wine
½ tsp. finely chopped fresh rosemary
½ tsp. finely chopped fresh thyme
1 to 2 tsp. fresh lemon juice
Kosher salt and freshly ground
  black pepper

In a 12-inch skillet, cook the bacon over medium heat until crisp, about 5 minutes. Transfer with a slotted spoon to a paper-towel-lined plate.

Add the chayote, onion, and garlic to the bacon fat in the skillet and toss to coat. Cook, covered, stirring occasionally, until the chayote and onion begin to brown slightly, about 10 minutes.

Add the wine, rosemary, and thyme; continue to cook, covered, stirring occasionally, until the chayote is tender, about 8 minutes more.

Remove from the heat, stir in the bacon, and season to taste with the lemon juice, salt, and pepper. Serve.

honey-roasted radishes

SERVES 4

1¾ lb. radishes (about 2 bunches),
  tops removed and reserved
2 Tbs. honey
1 Tbs. unsalted butter, melted
1 Tbs. white balsamic vinegar
Kosher salt and freshly ground black
  pepper

Position a rack in the center of the oven, set a 12-inch ovenproof skillet (preferably cast iron) on the rack, and heat the oven to 450°F.

Trim the radishes and then halve or quarter them lengthwise, depending on their size. Trim and discard the stems from the tops, wash the leaves thoroughly, and pat dry or dry in a salad spinner.

In a medium bowl, combine the honey, butter, vinegar, ½ tsp. salt, and ½ tsp. pepper. Add the radishes and toss until coated. Transfer to the hot skillet, spread in a single layer, and roast, stirring occasionally, until the radishes are crisp-tender, 15 to 20 minutes. Remove from the oven, add the radish leaves, and toss until the leaves are just wilted; serve.

roasted asparagus with chipotle-lime butter

SERVES 6 TO 8

2 lb. medium-thick asparagus,
  trimmed
2 Tbs. extra-virgin olive oil
1 medium lime, finely grated to yield
  2 tsp. zest; squeezed to yield
  2 Tbs. juice
Kosher salt and freshly ground black
  pepper

4 Tbs. unsalted butter, cut into
  8 pieces
2 tsp. finely chopped canned
  chipotle chile in adobo, plus 2 tsp.
  adobo sauce
1 Tbs. finely chopped fresh cilantro

Position racks in the upper and lower thirds of the oven, set a large rimmed baking sheet on each rack, and heat the oven to 425°F.

In a large bowl, toss the asparagus with the oil, lime zest, 1 tsp. salt, and ½ tsp. ground pepper. Divide the asparagus between the two hot baking sheets and roast, switching the positions of the pans halfway through, until tender and slightly browned in spots, 9 to 11 minutes.

Meanwhile, in a 1-quart saucepan, stir the butter, chipotle, adobo sauce, and ¾ tsp. salt over medium heat until the butter is melted. Remove from the heat and whisk in the lime juice and cilantro.

Transfer the asparagus to a platter, drizzle with the chipotle butter sauce, and serve.

peas and carrots with lemon, dill & mint

SERVES 8

1 to 2 medium lemons
½ cup extra-virgin olive oil
1 Tbs. minced fresh mint
1 tsp. minced fresh dill
Kosher salt and freshly ground
    black pepper

2 bunches small young carrots,
    preferably with tops (about 2 lb.)
8 oz. fresh sugar snap peas, trimmed
    and strings removed

Finely grate ½ tsp. zest from a lemon and then juice the lemon to yield ¼ cup (if it yields less, juice the second lemon). In a large bowl, whisk the zest, juice, oil, mint, dill, ½ tsp. salt, and ⅛ tsp. pepper.

Trim the tips and all but about ½ inch of the greens from the carrots and then peel them. In a large pot fitted with a steamer insert, bring an inch of water to a boil over high heat. Have ready a large bowl of ice water. Lay the carrots in the basket of the steamer, cover tightly, and steam until crisp-tender, 4 to 5 minutes. Cool the carrots in the ice water for a few minutes; then lift them out and add to the dressing.

Steam the peas in the same pot until tender, about 3 minutes. Cool them in the ice water for a few minutes, drain, and add to the carrots. Stir to coat the vegetables in the dressing. Add more salt, if needed.

Let the vegetables sit for at least 30 minutes and up to 1 hour, tossing occasionally. With a slotted spoon, transfer the vegetables to a serving platter. Serve chilled or at room temperature.

apple-rhubarb crisp

SERVES 8

For the topping
1 cup unbleached all-purpose flour
⅔ cup packed brown sugar
3 Tbs. granulated sugar
¼ cup finely chopped toasted
    almonds or walnuts
½ tsp. ground cinnamon
8 Tbs. butter, slightly softened and
    cut into small pieces

For the filling
2 lb. crisp baking apples (such as
    Gravensteins or Sierra Beauties),
    peeled, cored, and quartered
1½ lb. rhubarb, trimmed
1 to 1½ cups granulated sugar
4 Tbs. unbleached all-purpose flour
1 tsp. ground cinnamon

Position a rack the center of the oven and heat the oven to 350°F.

Make the topping

Mix together the flour, both sugars, nuts, and cinnamon in a large bowl.
Work in the butter until the mixture just holds together.

Make the filling, assemble & bake

Cut each of the apple quarters into 4 chunks; you should have about
5 cups. Cut the rhubarb into 1-inch-long pieces ½ inch wide; you should
have about 5 cups. In a large bowl, toss the apples and rhubarb with
the sugar, flour, and cinnamon until well coated. Transfer the apple and
rhubarb mixture to a 2-quart baking dish and sprinkle the topping over
the top. Bake until the topping is golden-brown and the fruit is bubbling,
1 hour to 1 hour, 15 minutes. Cool slightly before serving.

fresh berry pavlova

SERVES 6 TO 8

For the meringue shell

1¼ cups plus 2 tsp. superfine sugar

2 tsp. cornstarch

4 large egg whites, at room temperature

2 tsp. fresh lemon juice or white distilled vinegar

½ tsp. pure vanilla extract

¼ tsp. table salt

For the filling

2 pints mixed fresh berries or hulled, sliced strawberries (about 4 cups)

3 Tbs. granulated superfine sugar

2 Tbs. orange liqueur, such as Cointreau®

1¼ cups heavy cream

1 tsp. pure vanilla extract

¼ cup plain Greek-style yogurt

Make the shell

Position a rack in the lower third of the oven and heat the oven to 275°F. Line a baking sheet with parchment. Draw an 8-inch circle in the center of the parchment and then turn the paper over (you'll still see the circle).

Mix 2 tsp. of the sugar with the cornstarch and set it aside.

In a stand mixer fitted with the whisk attachment (or in a large bowl using a handheld electric mixer), beat the egg whites on medium-high speed until soft peaks form, about 2 minutes.

With the mixer running, slowly add the remaining 1¼ cups sugar, about 1 Tbs. at a time, taking 2 to 3 minutes to add it. Sprinkle in the cornstarch-sugar mixture, then add the lemon juice, vanilla, and salt. Continue beating until glossy stiff peaks form, another 1 to 2 minutes.

Pile the meringue onto the parchment circle and use an offset spatula or the back of a spoon to spread it into an 8-inch round, about 2½ inches high around the edge with a slightly concave center.

Put the meringue in the oven and turn the heat down to 250°F. Bake until crisp, dry, and slightly colored on the outside, about 45 minutes. (The meringue will spread a little during baking.) Rotate the baking sheet and continue baking until the meringue is hard on the outside and slightly darker, about 45 minutes more. Turn off the heat and leave the meringue in the oven to dry for at least 30 minutes. Cool completely and gently peel off the parchment. Don't worry if there are cracks or the center caves in slightly.

Make the filling

Combine the berries with 2 Tbs. of the sugar and the orange liqueur in a medium bowl. Let stand at room temperature, stirring occasionally, until the berries release their juice, about 45 minutes.

In a large bowl, beat the cream, the remaining 1 Tbs. sugar, and the vanilla with an electric mixer, increasing the speed from medium high to high as you beat, until soft peaks form, 2 to 3 minutes. Fold in the yogurt.

Carefully transfer the shell to a serving plate. Just before serving, fill the center with the cream and top with the berries. Use a serrated knife to slice the pavlova into wedges and serve.

strawberry-rhubarb fool

SERVES 4 TO 6

¾ lb. rhubarb, trimmed and sliced into ½-inch-thick pieces (about 2½ cups)
¾ cup granulated sugar
7 oz. strawberries, hulled and thinly sliced (1 heaping cup)
Fine sea salt or table salt
¾ cup heavy cream
1 Tbs. confectioners' sugar
½ tsp. rose water (optional)

Toss the rhubarb with ½ cup of the granulated sugar in a 2-quart saucepan. In a small bowl, toss the strawberries with the remaining ¼ cup sugar. Let sit, stirring each occasionally, until the sugar dissolves and juice begins to collect, about 30 minutes. Add the strawberry juice and a pinch of salt to the rhubarb, and stir to combine. Cook over medium heat, stirring occasionally, until the rhubarb is falling apart, about 10 minutes. Remove the pan from the heat, stir in the strawberries, and transfer the compote to a bowl. Refrigerate, uncovered, until cold, about 1½ hours. (To speed the chilling, stir the compote over a bowl of ice water until cold, about 20 minutes.)

tip

A little rose water adds a floral sweetness to this simple old-fashioned English dessert, but the fool is lovely without it, too.

In a chilled metal bowl, whisk the cream and confectioners' sugar until soft peaks form. Add the rose water, if using, and continue whipping to medium peaks. Set aside ⅓ cup of the cold strawberry-rhubarb compote, and fold the rest into the whipped cream just until the mixture looks streaky. Spoon into six glasses or dessert bowls and refrigerate for at least 1 hour before serving. (Refrigerate the remaining compote, too.) Serve topped with the remaining compote.

poached cherries

YIELDS 2½ CUPS

1¾ cups water
⅔ cup sugar
3 strips lemon zest, 1x3 inches each
3 strips orange zest, 1x3 inches each
¼ vanilla bean, split but not scraped

15 peppercorns
1 lb. fresh sweet cherries, rinsed and
  pitted

In a saucepan, bring the water, sugar, citrus zest, vanilla bean, and peppercorns to a boil, stirring to dissolve the sugar. Add the cherries and simmer until they're soft but not falling apart, about 10 minutes. Skim any foam from the surface. Let cool and then refrigerate. Strain the poaching liquid before serving.

tip

Pitted, poached cherries will keep in the refrigerator for a few weeks, ready to be spooned over ice cream.

strawberry-yogurt brûlée

SERVES 4

2 cups plain whole-milk Greek yogurt
1 cup coarsely chopped
   strawberries, plus several
   strawberry slices, for garnish
5 Tbs. turbinado or granulated sugar

In a medium bowl, combine the yogurt with the chopped strawberries and 1 Tbs. sugar. Divide among four 6-oz. ramekins. Garnish each with a few strawberry slices. Sprinkle each with about 1 Tbs. sugar. Pass the flame of a torch over the sugar until it's melted and browned, about 30 seconds. Serve immediately.

cherry, mango, kiwi & mint salad

YIELDS 6 CUPS

1 lb. fresh sweet cherries, rinsed and pitted

2 large ripe mangos, cut into ¾- to 1-inch chunks

2 kiwis, peeled, each cut into 8 lengthwise wedges and wedges cut in half crosswise

12 large mint leaves, cut in a chiffonade (stacked, rolled, and thinly sliced crosswise)

½ cup dessert wine, such as Muscat de Beaumes-de-Venise

2 Tbs. light brown sugar

1 tsp. grated orange zest

Pinch kosher salt

Toss all the ingredients together and refrigerate for at least 2 hours and for as long as 6 hours.

Recipe Index

Thai-Style Stir-Fried Chicken and
   Basil, 51
Udon with Tofu and Stir-Fried
   Vegetables, 46–47

Sides

Fava Beans with Prosciutto, Mint &
   Garlic, 58
Fennel Slaw with Grapefruit, Cracked
   Pepper & Pistachios, 56
Glazed Carrots with Tarragon, 61
Honey-Roasted Radishes, 66
Japanese Spinach with Sesame and
   Soy, 64
Korean Pickled Radish, 57
Pea, Morel & Fiddlehead Ragout, 62
Peas and Carrots with Lemon, Dill &
   Mint, 68
Radish, Carrot & Edamame Stir-Fry, 63

Roasted Asparagus with Chipotle-Lime
   Butter, 67
Sautéed Asparagus with Butter and
   Parmesan, 59
Sautéed Chayote with Sweet Onion and
   Bacon, 65
Sautéed Spinach with Golden Raisins,
   Pine Nuts & Breadcrumbs, 60
Toasted Israeli Couscous Salad with
   Mint, Cucumber & Feta, 55

Desserts

Apple-Rhubarb Crisp, 69
Cherry, Mango, Kiwi & Mint Salad, 76
Fresh Berry Pavlova, 70–71
Poached Cherries, 74
Strawberry-Rhubarb Fool, 72–73
Strawberry-Yogurt Brûlée, 75

COOK FRESH YEAR-ROUND

WINTER

FROM

FINE COOKING

from the editors and contributors
of *fine cooking*

The Taunton Press

The Taunton Press
Inspiration for hands-on living®

The Taunton Press, Inc., 63 South Main Street
PO Box 5506, Newtown, CT 06470-5506
e-mail: tp@taunton.com

Copy editor: Nina Rynd Whitnah
Indexer: Heidi Blough
Jacket/Cover design: Stacy Wakefield Forte
Interior design: Stacy Wakefield Forte

Recipes from: Tamar Adler, Pamela Anderson, Jennifer Armentrout, Nadia
Arumugam, Julie Grimes Bottcher, Andrew Carmellini, Dina Cheney, Ronne Day,
Tasha DeSerio, Mindy Fox, Gale Gand, Dabney Gough, Rosa Jackson, Matthew
Jennings, Kirstine Kidd, Allison Ehri Kreitler, Lori Longbotham, Ivy Manning, Selma
Morrow, Nancy Oakes, Liz Pearson, Melissa Pellegrino, Julissa Roberts, Tony
Rosenfeld, Mark Scarbrough, Layla Schlack, Samantha Seneviratne, Joanne
Smart, Molly Stevens, David Tanis, Bruce Weinstein, Joanne Weir, Shelley
Wiseman

The following names/brands appearing in *Winter* are trademarks: Maldon®,
Old Bay®

Library of Congress Cataloging-in-Publication Data
CookFresh year-round : seasonal recipes from Fine cooking /author, editors of
   Fine cooking.
      pages cm
   Includes index.
   ISBN 978-1-63186-014-0
1. Seasonal cooking. 2. Cookbooks. lcgft I. Taunton's fine cooking. II. Title: Cook
   Fresh year-round.
   TX714.C65428 2015
   641.5'64--dc23
                        2014039388

Printed in China
10 9 8 7 6 5 4 3 2 1

winter

contents

smoked trout with apple and crème fraîche

SERVES 8 TO 12

2 medium sweet, firm apples
   (such as Gala or Pink Lady)
8 oz. smoked trout
3 Tbs. thinly sliced fresh chives
2 Tbs. roasted walnut oil

⅛ tsp. freshly ground black pepper
About ¼ cup crème fraîche
1 medium lemon

Stand the apples on a cutting board and slice twelve ⅛-inch-thick rounds from the sides (not counting the small outermost slices); cut each round in half and arrange in a single layer on a platter.

Remove the skin from the trout and flake the flesh. Toss with the chives, walnut oil, and black pepper.

Using your fingers, divide the trout mixture among the apple slices. Use a small spoon to top each with a dollop of crème fraîche. Finely grate the zest from the lemon over all and serve.

creamy crab and artichoke dip

YIELDS 3½ CUPS; SERVES 12 TO 14

8 oz. crème fraîche

4 oz. cream cheese, cubed

2 medium cloves garlic

9 oz. thawed frozen artichoke hearts, gently squeezed dry

⅓ oz. finely grated Parmigiano-Reggiano (⅓ cup using a rasp grater)

2 tsp. Old Bay® seasoning

2 tsp. fresh lemon juice

2 tsp. Worcestershire sauce

1 lb. crabmeat, picked through for shells, drained, and excess liquid squeezed out if canned, or lightly shredded if fresh

Kosher salt

Position a rack 6 inches from the broiler element and heat the broiler on high.

Heat the crème fraîche and cream cheese in a 10-inch ovenproof skillet or flameproof baking dish over medium heat, stirring occasionally, until melted and bubbling, about 3 minutes.

Meanwhile, in a food processor, chop the garlic. Add the artichoke hearts, Parmigiano-Reggiano, Old Bay, fresh lemon juice, and Worcestershire sauce; pulse until coarsely chopped. Stir the crab and the artichoke mixture into the hot crème fraîche mixture and season to taste with salt. Broil until browned, about 3 minutes; serve from the baking dish or skillet (with a kitchen towel wrapped around the handle).

arugula with hearts of palm, grapefruit & oil-cured olives

SERVES 4 AS AN APPETIZER

1 large Ruby Red grapefruit
¼ cup extra-virgin olive oil
1½ Tbs. Champagne vinegar
1 tsp. finely chopped fresh rosemary
¼ tsp. crushed red pepper flakes
Kosher salt and freshly ground
   black pepper
3 hearts of palm, rinsed, halved
   lengthwise, and cut on a diagonal
   into ¾-inch pieces (about ¾ cup)

¼ cup pitted black oil-cured olives,
   halved lengthwise
7 oz. arugula (preferably bunched),
   trimmed (about 5 loosely packed
   cups)
¼ cup loosely packed fresh flat-leaf
   parsley leaves

Finely grate ½ tsp. zest from the grapefruit; set aside. Slice just enough off the top and bottom of the grapefruit to expose the fruit. Stand the grapefruit on one cut end and slice away all of the peel and white pith. Working over a bowl, cut the segments away from the membranes, letting them fall into the bowl. Then, over another bowl, squeeze the membranes to get any remaining juice. Cut each segment into thirds.

In a small bowl, whisk 2 Tbs. of the reserved grapefruit juice and the zest with the oil, vinegar, rosemary, red pepper flakes, ¼ tsp. salt, and a pinch of pepper.

In a small bowl, mix the grapefruit segments, hearts of palm, and olives with 2 Tbs. of the dressing.

Toss the arugula and parsley in a large bowl with a generous pinch of salt and 3 Tbs. of the dressing. Portion the arugula onto four plates, top with the hearts of palm mixture, and drizzle with the remaining dressing, if you like.

tip

Harvested from the inner core of a certain kind of palm tree, hearts of palm are available canned or packed in glass jars. Rinsing prior to using helps remove some of the jarred flavor.

seared scallops with cucumber and jalapeño

SERVES 6

2 tsp. canola oil
6 dry-packed sea scallops
Kosher salt
1 small English (seedless) cucumber
½ medium lime

1 Tbs. finely chopped seeded
   jalapeño
12 leaves fresh cilantro

Chill a small tray and a medium serving plate in the freezer.

Heat the oil in a 10-inch heavy-duty skillet (preferably cast iron) over medium-high heat until shimmering hot. Meanwhile, remove the side muscle from the scallops, halve them horizontally to make 12 thin rounds, and pat dry. Season each with salt. Cook, flipping once, until just cooked through, 3 minutes total. Transfer to the cold tray and return it to the freezer while you prep the remaining ingredients. (Don't freeze for more than 15 minutes or the scallops will be too hard to eat.)

Slice twelve ⅛-inch-thick rounds from the cucumber and arrange on the chilled serving plate. Top each cucumber with a scallop. Squeeze the lime over the scallops, sprinkle with the jalapeño, and garnish each with 1 leaf of the cilantro. Serve right away.

spicy papaya salad

SERVES 6

1 medium (3- to 4-lb.) ripe papaya
½ small red onion, very thinly
    sliced (¾ cup)
¼ cup coarsely chopped fresh
    cilantro
2 Tbs. fresh lime juice
1 Tbs. extra-virgin olive oil

1 tsp. freshly grated ginger
½ to 1 tsp. minced fresh Thai bird
    or habanero chile
⅛ tsp. ground allspice (optional)
½ tsp. kosher salt

Cut the papaya in half lengthwise. Using a spoon, scoop out and discard the seeds. Cut each half lengthwise into ¾-inch strips. Using a sharp paring knife, peel the strips, removing the skin as well as all the firm, lighter-colored flesh next to it. Cut the fruit crosswise into ¾-inch chunks and put in a large bowl.

Add the remaining ingredients and toss to combine. Let sit for 10 minutes at room temperature to meld the flavors, and serve.

tip

This savory fruit salad is great with chicken, fish, or roast pork. The optional allspice is a nod to its Jamaican inspiration.

endive and watercress salad with apples and herbs

SERVES 4

4 medium heads Belgian endive
(about 1 lb. total)
1 medium shallot, finely diced
(⅓ cup)
1 Tbs. fresh lemon juice;
more as needed
1 Tbs. white-wine vinegar;
more as needed
Kosher salt and freshly ground
black pepper
6 Tbs. heavy cream
2 Tbs. extra-virgin olive oil
1 bunch watercress (about 4 oz.),
thick stems trimmed, cut into
3-inch sprigs (5 cups)

1 large crisp apple, such as Pink Lady
or Granny Smith, thinly sliced
1 Tbs. coarsely chopped fresh
tarragon
1 Tbs. chives, cut at an angle into
¼-inch lengths
1 Tbs. coarsely chopped fresh chervil
(optional)
1 Tbs. coarsely chopped fresh
flat-leaf parsley (optional)
⅓ cup almonds, toasted and
coarsely chopped

To prep the Belgian endives, pluck off any bruised or damaged outer leaves and then cut the heads in half lengthwise through the root ends. Holding your knife at an angle, cut the endives crosswise into 1-inch-thick slices. Discard the root ends.

Combine the shallots, lemon juice, vinegar, and a pinch of salt in a small bowl. Let sit for 5 to 10 minutes. Whisk in the cream and olive oil, and season with a few grinds of pepper. Taste with a piece of endive and season the vinaigrette with more lemon juice, vinegar, or salt if necessary. Set aside.

Put the endives, watercress, apple, tarragon, chives, chervil (if using), and parsley (if using) in a large bowl. Season with salt and pepper. Gently toss the salad with just enough of the vinaigrette to lightly coat. Season to taste with more salt if necessary. Gently transfer the salad to a platter or individual serving plates. Scatter the almonds on top and serve, passing any remaining vinaigrette at the table.

shaved salad with spiced maple vinaigrette

SERVES 4 TO 6

3 Tbs. grade B pure maple syrup

½ cinnamon stick

2 whole allspice berries

1 small whole clove

1 whole star anise

½ tsp. grated peeled fresh ginger

2 Tbs. apple-cider vinegar

⅓ cup neutral oil, such as grape-
    seed or vegetable

Kosher salt and freshly ground
    black pepper

5 oz. (5 packed cups) mesclun
    salad mix

5 oz. head frisée, trimmed and
    torn into bite-size pieces

1 small turnip

1 small carrot

1 small parsnip

¼ cup shelled sunflower seeds,
    toasted

4 oz. aged sharp Cheddar,
    crumbled

Combine the maple syrup, cinnamon, allspice, clove, star anise, ginger, and 1 Tbs. water in a 1-quart saucepan. Simmer on medium-low heat to infuse the flavors and thicken slightly, about 3 minutes. Stir in the vinegar, then strain through a fine-mesh sieve into a medium bowl. Whisk in the oil in a slow stream, and season to taste with salt and pepper. Set aside and allow the vinaigrette to cool to room temperature.

Combine the mesclun and frisée in a large bowl. Peel the turnip, carrot, and parsnip. Using the peeler, shave each into thin ribbons into the bowl. Add the sunflower seeds and half of the cheese.

Whisk the vinaigrette, toss with the salad, and serve sprinkled with the remaining cheese.

celery root rémoulade

SERVES 4

6 cornichons or sour gherkins
¼ cup lightly packed fresh
   flat-leaf parsley
2 Tbs. fresh tarragon
1 anchovy fillet (optional)
¼ cup mayonnaise
¼ cup sour cream

2 Tbs. fresh lemon juice
1 Tbs. Dijon mustard
1 tsp. grated lemon zest
1 large celery root (also known
   as celeriac; about 1¼ lb.)
Kosher salt and freshly ground
   black pepper

In a food processor, pulse the cornichons, parsley, tarragon, and anchovy (if using) until coarsely chopped.

Add the mayonnaise, sour cream, lemon juice, mustard, and zest and process until well combined. Scrape the dressing into a large bowl.

Fit the processor with a medium grating disk. Peel the celery root with a knife (rather than a vegetable peeler) and cut it into chunks small enough to fit into the processor's feed tube. Grate the celery root in the processor.

Transfer the celery root to the bowl of dressing and fold gently to combine. Season to taste with salt and pepper and serve.

millet salad with avocado and citrus

SERVES 8 TO 10

1¾ cups millet
Kosher salt and freshly ground
  black pepper
½ cup plus 1 Tbs. extra-virgin
  olive oil; more as needed
3 Tbs. white-wine vinegar;
  more as needed
3 Tbs. grapefruit juice;
  more as needed

2 tsp. honey
¾ cup diced avocado (½-inch dice)
¾ cup orange segments,
  cut into pieces if large
¾ cup grapefruit segments,
  cut into pieces if large
¾ cup diced red onion (¼-inch dice)
¼ cup chopped fresh mint

Rinse the millet under cold water and drain. Bring 7 cups of water to a boil in a 4-quart pot over high heat. Add ¾ tsp. salt. Add the millet, reduce the heat to a simmer, and cook uncovered, stirring occasionally and adding more boiling water as necessary to keep the millet covered, until tender, 15 to 20 minutes. Drain and rinse the millet with cold water to stop the cooking.

Transfer the millet to a foil-lined rimmed baking sheet, drizzle with 1 Tbs. of the oil, and toss lightly to coat. Spread the millet on the baking sheet and cool completely at room temperature or in the refrigerator.

Put the vinegar and grapefruit juice in a small bowl and gradually whisk in the remaining ½ cup of oil. Whisk in the honey. Taste and season with salt, pepper, and additional vinegar, juice, or oil as needed.

Put the cooked and cooled millet in a large serving bowl and toss to break up any clumps. Add the avocado, orange segments, grapefruit segment, red onion, mint, and ½ cup vinaigrette and toss. Taste and season as needed with more vinaigrette, salt, and pepper, and serve.

tip

This salad can be refrigerated for up to 1 day. If making ahead, let sit at room temperature so it's not refrigerator-cold and season with more vinaigrette, salt, and pepper before serving.

shaved fennel salad with toasted almonds, lemon & mint

SERVES 4 TO 6

2 large fennel bulbs
   (about 4 lb. total)
3 Tbs. fresh lemon juice
Kosher salt and freshly ground
   black pepper

½ cup sliced almonds, toasted
¼ cup fresh mint leaves, torn
¼ cup extra-virgin olive oil

Trim the stalks from the fennel bulbs and remove the tough outer layer. Cut the bulbs in half lengthwise and core. Using a mandoline, shave the fennel crosswise; you'll have about 6 cups. (If you don't have a mandoline, quarter each bulb and use a vegetable peeler to shave them lengthwise.)

In a medium bowl, toss the fennel with the lemon juice and ½ tsp. salt and let sit for 10 minutes. Add half of the almonds and mint and all of the olive oil and toss to combine. Transfer the salad to a platter or divide it among serving plates. Scatter the remaining almonds and mint over the top, finish with a few grinds of pepper, and serve.

parsnip rémoulade

SERVES 4

1 lb. medium parsnips
   (about 5)
2 Tbs. white-wine vinegar
Kosher salt and freshly ground
   black pepper

⅓ cup crème fraîche
2 Tbs. extra-virgin olive oil
1½ tsp. drained capers, coarsely
   chopped

Peel the parsnips, then shave them with a vegetable peeler into long, thin ribbons, discarding the core; you'll have about 3½ cups.

In a medium bowl, toss the parsnips with the vinegar and 1 tsp. salt and let sit for 10 minutes.

Drain the parsnips in a colander and squeeze out as much vinegar as possible. Transfer to a medium bowl; add the crème fraîche, olive oil, and capers and toss to combine. Season to taste with salt and pepper and serve.

tip

✖ Parsnips tend to absorb a lot of the vinegar, so be sure to squeeze some of it out before dressing them.

roasted butternut squash salad with pears and stilton

SERVES 4

1 large butternut squash
   (about 3 lb.)
5 Tbs. extra-virgin olive oil
½ tsp. chopped fresh rosemary
Kosher salt and freshly ground
   black pepper
6 slices thick-cut bacon, cut into
   ½-inch pieces
1½ Tbs. balsamic vinegar

1 tsp. Dijon mustard
1 medium head escarole
   (about 1 lb.), trimmed and torn
   into 1½-inch pieces (about
   10 lightly packed cups)
2 medium firm-ripe pears
   (Bartlett or Anjou), peeled,
   cored, and sliced ⅛ inch thick
6 oz. Stilton, cut into 8 wedges

Position a rack in the center of the oven and heat the oven to 450°F.

Cut off the narrow top portion of the squash close to where it widens (reserve the base for another use). Peel and slice it into 12 thin (about ¼-inch) rounds.

Brush both sides of the squash with 1 Tbs. of the oil and spread in a single layer on a large rimmed baking sheet. Sprinkle with the rosemary, ½ tsp. salt, and ½ tsp. pepper. Roast, turning once, until softened and browned, about 25 minutes.

Meanwhile, in a 12-inch skillet, cook the bacon over medium heat, stirring occasionally, until crisp, 5 to 7 minutes. Transfer with a slotted spoon to paper towels to drain.

In a small bowl, whisk together the vinegar, mustard, ½ tsp. salt, and ½ tsp. pepper. Slowly whisk in the remaining 4 Tbs. oil and season with more salt and pepper to taste.

In a large bowl, toss the escarole and pears with enough of the vinaigrette to coat lightly. Season to taste with salt and pepper. Arrange the squash on four large dinner plates. Top each with a mound of the escarole and pears and sprinkle with the bacon. Tuck 2 wedges of Stilton into each salad and serve.

shaved rutabaga and turnip salad with scallions

SERVES 4

1 small rutabaga (1 lb.)
2 medium turnips
    (about 10 oz. total)
1 Tbs. rice vinegar
¼ tsp. Dijon mustard
½ tsp. kosher salt

2 medium scallions, trimmed
    and thinly sliced on the diagonal
    (keep white and green parts
    separate)
3 Tbs. extra-virgin olive oil
1 Tbs. coarsely chopped fresh
    flat-leaf parsley

Trim the root and stem ends from the rutabaga, peel it, and cut it lengthwise into 1-inch-thick slabs. Trim and peel the turnips. Using the vegetable peeler, shave enough rutabaga and turnip to measure 2 cups of each.

In a medium bowl, stir together the vinegar, mustard, and salt. Add the rutabaga, toss, and let sit for 15 minutes. Add the turnip and the white parts of the scallions, toss, and let sit for another 5 minutes. Add the olive oil, parsley, and the green parts of the scallions, toss gently, and serve.

smoked salmon and leek chowder

SERVES 4

3 Tbs. unsalted butter

2 medium leeks, white and
light green parts only, halved
lengthwise, thinly sliced, and
rinsed well (about 1 cup)

1 large rib celery, thinly sliced
(about ⅓ cup)

¼ cup unbleached all-purpose flour

2 cups whole milk

Two 8-oz. bottles clam juice

3 small red potatoes, cut into
½-inch dice (about 2½ cups)

1 bay leaf

6 oz. hot-smoked salmon,
skin and bones removed,
flaked into bite-size pieces
(about 1¼ cups)

½ cup heavy cream

2 Tbs. chopped fresh dill

1 Tbs. fresh lemon juice

Kosher salt and freshly ground
black pepper

Melt the butter in a 4-quart saucepan over medium heat. Add the leeks
and celery, and cook, stirring, until tender, about 6 minutes. Add the
flour and cook, stirring, for 1 minute.

Slowly whisk in the milk and clam juice, and bring to a simmer. Add
the potatoes and bay leaf, and simmer gently until the potatoes are
tender, about 12 minutes.

Add the salmon, cream, dill, and lemon juice, and cook until heated
through, about 1 minute. Season with salt and pepper, and serve.

cheddar and cauliflower soup

SERVES 6 TO 8

Kosher salt and freshly ground
　black pepper
½ head cauliflower (about 1 lb.),
　cored and cut into 1½-inch florets
2 Tbs. unsalted butter
1 medium yellow onion, small diced
1 medium clove garlic, minced
2 Tbs. unbleached all-purpose flour

¼ tsp. packed freshly grated nutmeg
⅛ tsp. cayenne
2 cups lower-salt chicken broth
½ cup heavy cream
3 sprigs fresh thyme
4 cups grated sharp or extra-sharp
　white Cheddar (about 14 oz.)

Bring a large pot of salted water to a boil. Boil the cauliflower until tender, about 4 minutes. Drain and let cool slightly. Trim the stems from 18 of the cauliflower pieces and cut the crowns into mini florets about ½ inch wide; set aside. Reserve the trimmed stems with the remaining larger pieces.

Melt the butter in a 4-quart saucepan over medium-low heat. Add the onion and ¼ tsp. salt and cook, stirring frequently, until soft, 10 to 12 minutes.

Add the garlic and cook until the aroma subsides, 2 to 3 minutes. Increase the heat to medium, and add the flour, nutmeg, and cayenne; cook for 3 minutes, stirring constantly. Whisk in the broth, cream, and 2 cups water. Add the thyme and bring to a simmer. Stir in the cheese until melted and simmer for 5 minutes to develop the flavors.

Remove and discard the thyme stems and stir in the larger cauliflower pieces and reserved stems. Working in batches, purée the soup in a blender. Return the soup to the pot, and season with salt and black pepper to taste. Add the mini cauliflower florets and reheat gently before serving.

tip

To dress up this rustic soup, garnish with a combination of 3 Tbs. toasted chopped walnuts, 1 Tbs. chopped fresh parsley, and 1½ tsp. finely grated lemon zest.

asian turkey noodle soup with bok choy

SERVES 4

4 oz. thin uncooked glass noodles

4 cups lower-salt chicken or turkey broth

3 large cloves garlic, smashed and peeled

One 2-inch-long piece of fresh ginger, peeled and thinly sliced, slices smashed

1½ Tbs. soy sauce; more for serving

1 medium head bok choy (about 8 oz.), sliced ¼ inch thick crosswise (about 3 cups)

2 cups coarsely shredded cooked turkey or chicken

2 scallions (white and green parts), thinly sliced

Put the noodles in a large bowl and cover with hot tap water; let soak while you prepare the other ingredients.

In a 3-quart saucepan, bring the broth, garlic, ginger, and soy sauce to a rapid simmer over medium-high heat. Cover and continue to simmer for 10 minutes; remove and discard the garlic and ginger.

Add the glass noodles to the broth and cook until nearly transparent (you should see only a tiny thread of white in the center of each noodle), about 4 minutes. Using tongs, distribute the noodles among four bowls.

Add the bok choy to the broth and cook, uncovered, just until the white parts start to become tender, 3 to 4 minutes. With a slotted spoon, remove the bok choy and distribute among the bowls.

Add the turkey to the broth and simmer just until heated through, about 30 seconds. Distribute the turkey and broth among the bowls. Top with the scallions and serve with more soy sauce on the side.

tip

Glass noodles are also known as cellophane noodles, bean threads, and bean vermicelli. They can be found dried in Asian specialty markets or in the Asian foods section of the supermarket. When cooked, they absorb sauces and broths well.

spicy sausage, escarole & white bean stew

SERVES 3 TO 4

1 Tbs. extra-virgin olive oil
1 medium yellow onion, chopped
¾ lb. hot Italian sausage, casings removed
2 medium cloves garlic, minced
Two 15-oz. cans cannellini beans, rinsed and drained

1 small head escarole, chopped into 1- to 2-inch pieces, washed, and lightly dried
1 cup low-salt canned chicken broth
1½ tsp. red-wine vinegar; more to taste
Kosher salt
¼ cup freshly grated Parmigiano-Reggiano

Heat the oil in a heavy 5- to 6-qt. Dutch oven over medium heat. Add the onion and cook, stirring occasionally, until tender, 5 to 6 minutes. Add the sausage, raise the heat to medium high, and cook, stirring and breaking up the sausage with a wooden spoon or spatula, until lightly browned and broken into small (1-inch) pieces, 5 to 6 minutes. Add the garlic and cook for 1 minute, then stir in the beans. Add the escarole to the pot in batches; using tongs, toss with the sausage mixture to wilt the escarole and make room for more.

When all the escarole is in, add the chicken broth, cover the pot, and cook until the beans are heated through and the escarole is tender, about 8 minutes. Season to taste with vinegar and salt. Transfer to bowls and sprinkle with some of the Parmigiano.

vegetable-miso soup

SERVES 4 TO 6

One 6 x 1-inch strip kombu
    (dried kelp)
2 Tbs. extra-virgin olive oil
1 cup thinly sliced leeks, white and
    light green parts only (from
    2 medium leeks), well rinsed
1 Tbs. finely chopped fresh ginger
2 tsp. finely chopped garlic
Pinch red pepper flakes (optional)

1 medium carrot, thinly sliced
    (¾ cup)
1 medium sweet potato, peeled
    and cut into bite-size pieces
    (about 2 cups)
8 oz. kale, trimmed and coarsely
    chopped (about 3 cups)
½ cup red (aka) miso
1 Tbs. mirin; more to taste

In a 3- to 4-quart saucepan, bring 6 cups water and the kombu to a simmer over medium heat. Reduce the heat to low and cook for 1 minute. Discard the kombu and transfer the dashi to a large measuring cup or bowl. Dry the saucepan.

Heat the oil in the saucepan over medium heat. Add the leeks and cook, stirring, until slightly softened, about 2 minutes. Add the ginger, garlic, and pepper flakes (if using), and cook until fragrant, 1 to 2 minutes. Add the carrot and sweet potato and cook until slightly softened, 3 to 4 minutes. Add the dashi, turn the heat up to medium high, and bring to a boil. Add the kale and simmer until all of the vegetables are tender, 5 to 7 minutes.

Transfer ¼ cup of the dashi to a small bowl and whisk in the miso until dissolved. Add to the soup and simmer for 1 minute. Add the mirin, seasoning with more to taste, and serve.

spinach and chickpea curry

SERVES 4

3 Tbs. canola oil
¼ medium red onion, thinly sliced
2 Tbs. finely chopped fresh ginger
1 Tbs. curry powder
1 tsp. garam masala
⅛ tsp. cayenne
One 15-oz. can chickpeas, rinsed and drained

One 14½-oz. can diced tomatoes
Kosher salt
7 oz. (7 packed cups) baby spinach
¼ cup chopped fresh cilantro
½ cup Greek yogurt

Heat the oil in a 12-inch sauté pan over medium-high heat. Add the onion, ginger, curry powder, garam masala, and cayenne, and cook, stirring often, until the onion is softened, 2 to 3 minutes. Stir in the chickpeas, tomatoes, and 1¼ tsp. salt. Add the spinach by the handful, stirring to wilt it as you go. Continue to cook, stirring often, until the spinach is completely wilted and the flavors have melded, 4 to 5 minutes more. Season to taste with more salt. Remove the pan from the heat and stir in the cilantro.

Spoon onto a platter, and serve with the yogurt for dolloping on top.

shrimp tacos with spicy cabbage slaw

SERVES 2

¼ cup mayonnaise

1 Tbs. plus 2 tsp. fresh lime juice, plus lime wedges, for serving

1 tsp. minced chipotles in adobo

¼ cup chopped fresh cilantro

One 5-oz. package classic coleslaw mix (about 2½ cups)

Four 6- to 7-inch corn tortillas

2 Tbs. vegetable oil

10 oz. medium (41 to 50 per lb.) easy-to-peel shrimp, peeled and deveined

Kosher salt

In a medium bowl, mix the mayonnaise, 2 tsp. lime juice, and minced chipotles in adobo. Stir in the chopped cilantro and coleslaw mix.

Heat a heavy-duty 12-inch skillet over medium heat. One at a time, heat four 6- to 7- inch tortillas, flipping once, until softened, about 30 seconds per side. Wrap in a clean dishtowel to keep warm.

Heat the vegetable oil in the skillet over medium heat until shimmering hot. Add the shrimp, season with salt, and cook, stirring, until just opaque throughout, about 2 minutes. Remove from the heat and drizzle with the remaining 1 Tbs. fresh lime juice. Wrap the shrimp and slaw in the warm tortillas. Serve with lime wedges on the side.

tip

✕ Packaged coleslaw mix saves prep time for this fresh-tasting taco. Buying peeled shrimp, if you can find it, would save a step, too.

crispy flounder with pears, endive & meyer lemon

SERVES 4

2 small Meyer lemons

6 Tbs. unsalted butter

3 medium Belgian endive, trimmed and quartered lengthwise

3 medium firm-ripe pears, peeled, cored, and sliced lengthwise ½ inch thick

Kosher salt and freshly ground black pepper

½ Tbs. thinly sliced chives; more for garnish

½ cup unbleached all-purpose flour

½ cup fine-ground cornmeal

4 small flounder or sole fillets (about 1½ lb.)

2 Tbs. olive oil

½ cup dry white wine

Finely grate 2 tsp. zest from one of the lemons. Squeeze 1½ lemons to yield 2 Tbs. of juice. Thinly slice the remaining lemon half and cut each slice into quarters; set aside.

In a 10- to 11-inch straight-sided sauté pan, melt 3 Tbs. of the butter over medium heat until foamy. Add the endive, pears, lemon juice, lemon zest, and ½ tsp. salt; stir to combine. Cover, reduce the heat to medium low, and cook, stirring occasionally until tender, 15 to 20 minutes. Remove the lid and cook until the endive and pears are lightly browned in places, about 2 minutes. Remove from the heat and stir in the chives.

While the endive and pears cook, combine the flour and cornmeal in a shallow dish. Season the fish lightly with salt and pepper and then dredge it in the cornmeal mixture. Heat ½ Tbs. of the butter with 1 Tbs. of the oil in a 12-inch skillet over medium-high heat. Cook 2 of the fillets, flipping once, until golden brown and cooked through, 2 to 3 minutes per side. Transfer to a clean plate. Wipe out the skillet and repeat with another ½ Tbs. butter and the remaining 1 Tbs. oil and fillets. Transfer to the plate with the other fish. Wipe out the skillet again.

Heat the remaining 2 Tbs. butter in the pan until melted and browned and then stir in the lemon slices and a pinch of salt. Add the wine, bring to a simmer, and reduce by half, 1 to 2 minutes. Season to taste with salt and pepper.

Portion the pear mixture onto four dinner plates and top each with a fillet. Spoon the lemon pan sauce over the fish, garnish with chives, and serve.

shrimp and pineapple stir-fry with coconut rice

SERVES 4

1⅓ cups jasmine rice

¾ cup canned unsweetened coconut milk

Kosher salt and freshly ground black pepper

⅓ cup golden rum

⅓ cup fresh lime juice (from 3 medium limes); more to taste

2 tsp. cornstarch

1¼ lb. jumbo shrimp (21 to 25 per lb.), preferably wild, peeled and deveined

2 Tbs. vegetable oil

Four ⅓-inch-thick rounds peeled, cored pineapple, each cut into 8 wedges

⅓ cup coarsely chopped fresh mint

In a microwave-safe 8- to 10-cup bowl, combine the rice, coconut milk, and ¾ tsp. salt with 2 cups water. Microwave on high power, uncovered, for 15 minutes. Let stand in the closed microwave until all the water is absorbed, at least 5 and up to 15 minutes.

Meanwhile, in a small bowl, whisk the rum, lime juice, cornstarch, ¼ tsp. salt, and ¼ tsp. pepper until the cornstarch dissolves.

Pat the shrimp dry and season with ¼ tsp. salt and ¼ tsp. pepper.

tip

You can speed up the prep work in this dish by buying peeled shrimp and precut pineapple. Cooking the rice in coconut milk adds just the right amount of sweetness.

Heat the oil in a wok or a 12-inch nonstick skillet over medium-high heat until shimmering hot, 1 to 2 minutes. Add the shrimp and stir-fry until partially cooked, about 2 minutes. Add the pineapple and continue to stir-fry until heated through, about 1 minute. Whisk the sauce, add it to the skillet, and stir until the shrimp are just opaque in the center and coated with the thickened sauce, about 1 minute. Stir in the mint and remove the wok from the heat.

Fluff the rice with a fork, spoon it onto four dinner plates, top with the stir-fry, and serve.

creamy orecchiette with spinach and prosciutto

Kosher salt and freshly ground
    black pepper
¾ lb. dried orecchiette or medium
    shells
8 oz. baby spinach leaves
    (about 8 lightly packed cups)
½ cup mascarpone

2 oz. coarsely grated Parmigiano-
    Reggiano (about 1 cup using a
    box grater)
1 tsp. finely grated lemon zest
2 oz. prosciutto (about 4 thin
    slices), coarsely chopped

Bring a 6- to 8-quart pot of well-salted water to a boil over high heat. Add the pasta and cook according to the package directions until al dente. Gently stir in the spinach and cook until wilted, a few seconds. Reserve ¼ cup of the cooking water and drain the pasta and spinach.

Return the pot to the stove over low heat, add the mascarpone, Parmigiano, and lemon zest and cook until the mascarpone has melted, about 1 minute. Add the pasta, spinach, reserved pasta water, and the prosciutto and toss gently. Season to taste with pepper and serve.

open-face brie, apple & arugula sandwiches

SERVES 4

8 slices rustic artisan bread
   (about 2½ by 6 inches and
   ¾ inch thick)
8 tsp. Dijon mustard
4 cups packed baby arugula
1 medium Fuji apple, cored
   and thinly sliced

Kosher salt and freshly ground
   black pepper
8 oz. Brie, thinly sliced

Position a rack 6 inches from the broiler and heat the broiler to high.

Put the bread slices on a rimmed baking sheet and set under the broiler. Broil until nicely toasted, 1 to 2 minutes.

Remove the pan from the oven, flip the bread over, and spread 1 tsp. of the mustard evenly on each untoasted side. Top with the arugula and then the apple slices. Season lightly with salt and pepper, and then arrange the Brie slices in a single layer over the apples.

Broil just until the Brie starts to melt, 1 to 2 minutes (don't let it melt too much or the apple will get warm and the arugula will wilt). Sprinkle with a little black pepper.

chicken burgers with red cabbage and apple slaw

SERVES 4

1 lb. ground chicken (not chicken breast)

1½ cups small-diced peeled Granny Smith apple (about 1 large)

½ cup small-diced red onion (about ½ medium)

¼ cup small-diced celery (about ½ rib)

5 Tbs. mayonnaise

2 tsp. Dijon mustard

2 tsp. minced garlic

Kosher salt and freshly ground black pepper

2 Tbs. vegetable oil

1 tsp. fresh lime juice; more as needed

1½ cups packed thinly sliced red cabbage

4 challah rolls or hamburger buns, split and toasted

In a medium bowl, combine the chicken with ½ cup of the apple, the onion, celery, 2 Tbs. of the mayonnaise, 1 tsp. of the mustard, the garlic, ½ tsp. salt, and ¼ tsp. pepper. Gently mix with your hands and form four ½-inch-thick patties. Make an indentation in the center of each one with your thumb.

In a 12-inch nonstick skillet, heat the vegetable oil over medium heat until shimmering hot. Cook the burgers until golden-brown on one side, about 5 minutes. Flip and continue cooking until the internal temperature reaches 165°F on an instant-read thermometer, 5 to 9 minutes more.

Meanwhile, in a medium bowl, mix the remaining 3 Tbs. mayonnaise and 1 tsp. mustard with the lime juice. Add the remaining apple, the cabbage, and ⅛ tsp. each salt and pepper; toss to combine. Season to taste with more lime juice, salt, and pepper.

Serve the burgers in the rolls, topped with the slaw.

tip

Red cabbage has slightly more peppery flavor than green or white cabbage. It provides great crunch with the chicken burgers, which are subtly sweet thanks to the addition of apples and celery.

portabella mushrooms with creamy spinach-artichoke filling

SERVES 4

3 Tbs. olive oil

3 medium cloves garlic, minced (1 Tbs.)

4 medium portabella mushrooms, stemmed, gills

Kosher salt and freshly ground black pepper

4 oz. cream cheese, softened

3 Tbs. mayonnaise

1½ tsp. fresh thyme

9 to 10 oz. frozen chopped spinach, thawed and squeezed dry

9 oz. frozen artichokes, thawed, lightly squeezed dry, and chopped

½ cup fresh breadcrumbs or panko

⅓ cup finely grated Parmigiano-Reggiano

Position a rack in the center of the oven and heat the oven to 450°F.

In a small bowl, combine 2 Tbs. of the oil and about two-thirds of the minced garlic. Brush the insides of the mushroom caps with the garlic oil and sprinkle generously with salt and pepper. Arrange the mushrooms oiled side up on a rimmed baking sheet and roast until just tender, about 10 minutes.

Meanwhile, in a medium bowl, mix the cream cheese, mayonnaise, and ½ tsp. of the thyme with the back of a wooden spoon. Stir in the spinach and artichokes and season to taste with salt and pepper. In another medium bowl, combine the remaining garlic, 1 Tbs. oil, and 1 tsp. thyme with the breadcrumbs and cheese.

Spoon the artichoke mixture evenly into the mushroom caps and sprinkle with the breadcrumb mixture. Bake until the crumbs are golden-brown and the filling is hot, about 10 minutes. Serve immediately.

tip

If you can't find frozen artichoke hearts, substitute a 14-oz. can of artichoke hearts, drained and patted dry.

sea scallops with brussels sprouts and mustard sauce

SERVES 2 TO 3

1 lb. dry-packed sea scallops,
   patted dry
10 oz. Brussels sprouts, trimmed
3 Tbs. olive oil
Kosher salt and freshly ground
   black pepper

Unbleached all-purpose flour,
   for dusting
2 Tbs. unsalted butter, cold,
   cut into pieces
1 Tbs. fresh lemon juice
1 tsp. coarse-grained Dijon mustard

Remove the side muscle from the scallops.

In a food processor fitted with the 2-mm slicing blade, shred the Brussels sprouts. Heat 2 Tbs. olive oil in a 12-inch nonstick skillet over medium-high heat until shimmering hot. Add the Brussels sprouts, season with salt and pepper, and toss to coat with the oil. Cover and cook until starting to soften, about 1½ minutes. Transfer to a platter and keep warm.

Season the scallops with salt and pepper. Dust both flat sides with all-purpose flour. Heat the remaining 1 Tbs. olive oil in the skillet over medium-high heat until shimmering hot. Add the scallops and cook, flipping once, until browned and just cooked through, about 5 minutes. Put the scallops on top of the Brussels sprouts and return the skillet to medium-low heat. Add the butter pieces, lemon juice, 2 Tbs. water, and the Dijon mustard and cook, stirring and scraping up any browned bits, until the butter is incorporated and the sauce has thickened, about 1 minute. Season to taste with salt and pepper, spoon over the scallops, and serve.

tip

Brussels sprouts have a slightly crunchy texture and subtly sweet flavor that complements scallops. When thinly sliced, they cook in just a couple of minutes.

pork chops with cranberry–maple pan sauce

SERVES 4

Four 1-inch-thick bone-in pork chops (about 2½ lb.)
2 tsp. chopped fresh thyme
Kosher salt and freshly ground black pepper
1½ Tbs. olive oil

1 cup fresh or frozen cranberries
½ cup lower-salt chicken broth
½ cup pure maple syrup
2 tsp. cider vinegar
2 tsp. Dijon mustard

Pat the pork dry and season with 1 tsp. of the thyme, 1¼ tsp. salt, and ¾ tsp. pepper.

Heat the oil in a heavy-duty 12-inch skillet over medium heat until shimmering hot. Add the pork chops and cook without moving until the pork is browned around the edges and easily releases when you lift a corner, 3 to 4 minutes. Flip the pork chops and continue to cook until firm to the touch and an instant-read thermometer inserted horizontally into a chop close to but not touching the bone registers 140°F, about 9 minutes.

Transfer the chops to a plate and cover loosely with foil to keep warm. Add the cranberries, chicken broth, maple syrup, cider vinegar, mustard, and the remaining 1 tsp. thyme to the skillet and raise the heat to medium high. Cook, whisking to incorporate the mustard and any browned bits from the bottom of the pan, until the cranberries soften and the liquid has reduced to a saucy consistency, about 7 minutes.

Return the pork chops and any accumulated juice to the skillet, turning to coat both sides. Serve the pork chops with the sauce.

tip

When buying fresh cranberries, choose plump, brightly colored berries. Store in the refrigerator for up to 4 weeks or freeze them for up to a year. If freezing, wash, dry, and pick through the berries first (discard any dark, mushy ones) and then transfer them to a heavy-duty freezer bag.

sear-roasted rib-eye with creamed chard

SERVES 4

1 tsp. Worcestershire sauce
Kosher salt and freshly ground
    black pepper
Two 1½-inch-thick boneless
    rib-eye steaks (2 lb. total),
    each cut into two equal pieces
    and patted dry
2½ Tbs. olive oil
2 large cloves garlic, minced

1½ lb. Swiss chard, washed, stems
    halved lengthwise and thinly
    sliced crosswise, leaves sliced
    into ribbons about ½ inch thick
1 tsp. chopped fresh thyme
2 Tbs. dry white wine
½ cup heavy cream
1½ tsp. fresh lemon juice; more
    to taste
¾ oz. finely grated Parmigiano-
    Reggiano (¾ cup)

Position a rack in the center of the oven and heat
the oven to 425°F. Set a wire rack over a rimmed
baking sheet lined with foil.

In a small bowl, combine the Worcestershire
sauce with 2 tsp. salt and ½ tsp. black pepper,
and rub all over the steaks.

Heat 1 Tbs. of the olive oil in a heavy-duty
12-inch skillet over medium-high heat until shimmering hot. Sear the steaks until well browned,
about 3 minutes per side. Transfer to the rack

tip

Any kind of chard will work well, but rainbow chard adds nice color.

and roast until medium rare (130°F), 8 to 10 minutes. Transfer to a platter, tent with foil, and let rest for at least 5 minutes.

While the steaks are in the oven, return the skillet to medium heat, add the remaining 1½ Tbs. oil and the garlic, and cook, stirring, until pale golden, about 1 minute. Add the chard stems, thyme, and a pinch of salt; cook, stirring occasionally, until just tender, about 5 minutes. In batches, add the chard leaves, tossing with tongs and ¼ tsp. salt, and cook until wilted, about 5 minutes. Transfer to a large sieve and press on the chard with the back of a spoon to drain as much liquid as possible.

Return the chard to the skillet over medium heat and add the wine. Cook, stirring occasionally, until the wine is almost evaporated, about 2 minutes. Add the cream, bring to a boil, then adjust the heat to simmer and cook until the cream is reduced by half, about 3 minutes. Off the heat, stir in the lemon juice and Parmigiano. Season to taste with more lemon juice, salt, and pepper. Serve with the steaks.

poached chicken and vegetables with thai peanut sauce

SERVES 4

1 cup well-shaken canned
  coconut milk

½ cup peanut butter, preferably
  natural

4 tsp. fish sauce

1 Tbs. Thai red curry paste

1 Tbs. packed dark brown sugar

1 Tbs. fresh lime juice; more to
  taste

5 oz. baby spinach leaves
  (about 5 cups)

¾ lb. broccoli crowns, cut into
  1-inch florets (about 4 cups)

2 large carrots, sliced diagonally
  ¼ inch thick (about ¾ cup)

1 lb. boneless, skinless chicken
  breasts, sliced crosswise into
  ½-inch-thick strips

1 tsp. kosher salt

Bring 6 cups water to a boil in a 6- to 8-quart pot. Have ready a metal steamer basket or bamboo steamer that fits the pot.

Meanwhile, whisk the coconut milk, peanut butter, fish sauce, curry paste, brown sugar, and lime juice in a 1-quart saucepan. Cook over medium heat, whisking frequently, until bubbly. Season to taste with lime juice and keep warm on low heat.

Cook the spinach in the water until wilted, about 1 minute. With a slotted spoon, transfer the spinach to a sieve and press on it to remove as much liquid as possible. Set aside.

Return the water to a boil. Fit the metal steamer basket or bamboo steamer into or over the pot. Arrange the broccoli and carrots in the steamer, cover, and steam until just tender, about 6 minutes. Remove the steamer from the pot.

Add the chicken and salt to the water. Turn off the heat, cover, and let the chicken poach until cooked through, about 5 minutes.

With a slotted spoon, transfer the chicken and vegetables to a platter, season to taste with salt and pepper, and serve with the sauce.

spicy korean-style pork medallions with asian slaw

SERVES 4 TO 6

1 large or 2 small pork tenderloins (about 1¼ lb.)
⅓ cup soy sauce
¼ cup rice vinegar
3 Tbs. light brown sugar
2 medium cloves garlic, minced
1½ Tbs. minced fresh ginger
1 Tbs. Asian sesame oil
1 Tbs. Asian chile sauce (like Sriracha)

1 lb. napa cabbage, thinly sliced (about 6 cups)
1 cup grated carrot (about 2 medium carrots)
4 scallions (white and green parts), trimmed and thinly sliced
5 Tbs. canola or peanut oil
Kosher salt

Trim the pork of any silverskin and excess fat, and cut on the diagonal into ½-inch-thick medallions.

In a small measuring cup, whisk together the soy sauce, 2 Tbs. of the rice vinegar, 2 Tbs. of the brown sugar, the garlic, ginger, ½ Tbs. of the sesame oil, and 2 tsp. of the chile sauce. Toss ½ cup of this mixture with the pork medallions in a large bowl; reserve the remaining mixture to use as a sauce. Let the pork sit at room temperature for 25 minutes or refrigerate for up to 2 hours.

Meanwhile, in another large bowl, toss the cabbage and the carrot with half of the scallions, 1 Tbs. of the canola oil, 1 tsp. salt, and the remaining 2 Tbs. rice vinegar, 1 Tbs. brown sugar, ½ Tbs. sesame oil, and 1 tsp. chile sauce. Let sit for 15 minutes, toss again, and transfer to a large serving platter.

Heat 2 Tbs. of the canola oil in a 12-inch, heavy-based skillet over medium-high heat until shimmering hot. Remove the pork from the marinade, shaking off the excess, and transfer the pork to a clean plate. Discard the marinade. Add half of the pork medallions to the skillet, spacing them without touching, and cook until well browned, about 2 minutes. Flip and cook until the pork is just cooked through (slice into a piece to check), about 2 more minutes. Set the pork on top of the slaw.

Pour out the oil and wipe the pan with paper towels (if the drippings on the bottom of the pan look like they may burn, wash the pan). Return the pan to medium-high heat. Add the remaining 2 Tbs. canola oil, and cook the remaining medallions in the same manner. Top the slaw with the remaining pork, and pour the reserved soy-ginger sauce over the medallions. Serve immediately, sprinkled with the remaining scallions.

maple-roasted butternut squash, chard & sausage flatbread

SERVES 4

1 lb. pizza dough, thawed if frozen

1 lb. butternut squash, peeled, halved lengthwise, seeded, and sliced crosswise ¼ inch thick

3 Tbs. pure maple syrup

2 Tbs. extra-virgin olive oil

Kosher salt and freshly ground black pepper

Semolina or cornmeal, for dusting the pan

½ small red onion, thinly sliced (¾ cup)

1 Tbs. fresh thyme, coarsely chopped

6 oz. fresh pork sausage (hot or sweet), removed from casings if necessary, crumbled

6 oz. fresh whole-milk ricotta (¾ cup)

¾ oz. finely grated pecorino romano (¾ cup using a rasp grater)

1 tsp. apple-cider vinegar

2 cups very thinly sliced rainbow chard leaves

Position a rack in the center of the oven and heat the oven to 450°F. Let the pizza dough stand at room temperature while you roast the squash.

In a large bowl, toss the squash with 2 Tbs. of the maple syrup, 1½ tsp. of the oil, ¼ tsp. salt, and ⅛ tsp. pepper. Spread it in a single layer on a large heavy-duty rimmed baking sheet and roast until tender and lightly browned, about 12 minutes. Let cool to warm.

Dust another large heavy-duty rimmed baking sheet with semolina or cornmeal. On a lightly floured work surface, roll the dough into a ¼-inch-thick oval; transfer to the prepared baking sheet.

Lower the oven temperature to 425°F.

In the large bowl, gently toss the squash, onion, thyme, 1½ tsp. of the remaining oil, ½ tsp. salt, and ¼ tsp. pepper.

Scatter the squash mixture evenly over the dough, then scatter the sausage and teaspoonfuls of ricotta all over. Sprinkle with the pecorino and bake until the crust is golden-brown and crisp, about 30 minutes.

In a large bowl, whisk the remaining 1 Tbs. syrup and 1 Tbs. oil, the vinegar, ½ tsp. salt, and ¼ tsp. pepper. Add the chard to the bowl, and toss to coat. Scatter the chard over the flatbread. Cut into pieces and serve.

shrimp and spinach salad with orange, avocado & pistachios

SERVES 4

¼ cup extra-virgin olive oil
1½ Tbs. sherry vinegar
½ cup finely chopped red onion
1 Tbs. finely grated orange zest
  (from 2 oranges)
Kosher salt and freshly ground
  black pepper
1 large firm-ripe Hass avocado,
  cut into ¾-inch pieces

5 oz. baby spinach (5 lightly
  packed cups)
1 lb. medium (41 to 50 per lb.)
  cooked easy-to-peel shrimp,
  peeled and deveined
¼ cup roasted, salted shelled
  pistachios

In a small bowl, slowly whisk the olive oil into the sherry vinegar. Whisk in the chopped onion and orange zest and season to taste with salt and black pepper.

Cut the white pith from the oranges and cut them in half lengthwise. Cut lengthwise again into ⅓-inch-thick slices. Holding the slices together, cut crosswise into thirds and put them in a large bowl. Add the avocado pieces to the bowl along with the baby spinach and cooked shrimp.

Whisk the vinaigrette and gently toss with the salad. Season to taste with salt and black pepper. Sprinkle with the pistachios.

seared tilapia with spicy orange salsa

SERVES 4

4 medium navel oranges (about 2 lb.)
½ cup small-diced red onion
½ cup coarsely chopped fresh cilantro
2 Tbs. fresh lime juice
1 tsp. ground cumin

Kosher salt and freshly ground black pepper
1 fresh serrano or jalapeño chile, minced (seeds included)
Four 5-oz. tilapia fillets
2 Tbs. mild olive oil

Using a sharp paring knife, cut off the ends of the oranges to expose a circle of flesh. Stand each orange on an end and pare off the rest of the peel, including all the white pith, in strips, following the curve of the orange. Working over a medium bowl, carefully cut on both sides of each orange segment to free it from the membranes. Then squeeze the membranes over the bowl to collect any remaining juice. Cut the segments crosswise into 4 pieces and return to the bowl.

Add the onion, cilantro, lime juice, cumin, and 1 tsp. salt and gently stir to combine. Add enough of the chile to suit your taste and stir. Let stand at room temperature for at least 10 minutes to meld the flavors.

Pat the fish dry and season with salt and pepper. Heat the oil in a 10-inch nonstick skillet over medium-high heat until shimmering hot. Cook 2 of the fillets, flipping once, until browned and just cooked through, 1½ to 2 minutes per side. Transfer to dinner plates. Repeat with the remaining fillets. Use a slotted spoon to top the fish with the salsa.

roasted cauliflower and goat cheese frittata

SERVES 4 TO 6

1 small red onion, halved and
   thinly sliced lengthwise
2 Tbs. distilled white vinegar
Kosher salt and freshly ground
   black pepper
2 cups 1-inch cauliflower florets
   (about ½ small head)

2 Tbs. plus 2 tsp. extra-virgin
   olive oil
8 large eggs
2 Tbs. chopped fresh dill
½ tsp. whole-grain mustard
2 Tbs. unsalted butter
6 oz. fresh goat cheese,
   crumbled (1⅓ cups)

Position a rack about 6 inches from the broiler and heat the broiler
on high.

Combine the onion, vinegar, and ½ tsp. salt in a small bowl; let sit for
10 minutes and then drain and pat the onion dry. Set aside.

Meanwhile, on a large rimmed baking sheet, toss the cauliflower with
2 tsp. of the oil, ½ tsp. salt, and ¼ tsp. pepper. Broil, tossing once or twice,
until the edges are golden, 3 to 6 minutes.

Reposition the rack in the center of the oven and set the oven
to 400°F.

Whisk the eggs, dill, mustard, ½ tsp. salt, and ½ tsp. pepper in a
medium bowl.

Heat the remaining 2 Tbs. oil and the butter in a 12-inch ovenproof
skillet over medium-high heat until the butter melts. Add the onion and

cook, stirring occasionally, until some of the pieces are dark golden brown, about 3 minutes. Remove the skillet from the heat, stir in the roasted cauliflower, and then slowly pour in the egg mixture, redistributing the vegetables evenly. Sprinkle the goat cheese on top and bake until the eggs are set in the center, about 10 minutes. Let rest for 5 minutes and then use a silicone spatula to slide the frittata onto a serving plate or cutting board. Slice into wedges and serve.

tip

When working with cauliflower, always start by trimming away the leaves and base of the stem. For whole florets, simply cut the floret away from the central stem with a knife, then cut them as needed in your recipe.

pasta with roasted cauliflower, arugula & prosciutto

SERVES 4

Kosher salt and freshly ground
   black pepper
½ medium head cauliflower,
   cored and cut into ¾-inch
   florets (3½ cups)
1 pint grape tomatoes
3 Tbs. extra-virgin olive oil
9 large fresh sage leaves

4 large cloves garlic, peeled
6 thin slices prosciutto
   (about 4 oz.)
12 oz. dried orecchiette
5 oz. baby arugula (5 lightly
   packed cups)
¾ cup grated Parmigiano-
   Reggiano

Position a rack in the lower third of the oven and heat the oven to 425°F.
Bring a large pot of well-salted water to a boil.

Toss the cauliflower, tomatoes, oil, ¾ tsp. salt, and ½ tsp. pepper
on a rimmed baking sheet; spread in a single layer. Roast, stirring once,
until the cauliflower turns golden and is tender, about 15 minutes.

Meanwhile, pulse the sage and garlic in a food processor until
minced. Add the prosciutto and pulse until coarsely chopped.

Toss the cauliflower with the herb mixture and continue to roast
until fragrant and the cauliflower is golden-brown, 5 to 7 minutes.

Boil the pasta until al dente, 9 to 10 minutes. Reserve 1 cup of pasta
water. Drain the pasta and return to the pot. Stir in the cauliflower, arugula, cheese, and pasta water to moisten. Season with salt and pepper.

parsnip, potato & scallion pancakes

YIELDS 8 TO 10 PANCAKES; SERVES 8

1 lb. russet potatoes, peeled
1 lb. medium parsnips, peeled
    and cored
¾ cup thinly sliced scallions
    (white and green parts)
2 large eggs, beaten

2 Tbs. unbleached all-purpose
    flour
Kosher salt and freshly ground
    black pepper
Vegetable oil, for the griddle

Using a food processor fitted with the medium grating disk, grate the potatoes and parsnips separately. Put the potatoes in a clean kitchen towel and squeeze out as much liquid as possible. In a large bowl, combine the potatoes, parsnips, scallions, eggs, flour, 2 tsp. salt, and a few grinds of pepper; mix well.

Generously oil a griddle and heat over medium heat. Working in batches, spoon about ⅓ cup of the mixture onto the griddle at a time to form pancakes. Flatten the pancakes with a spatula (they should be about ½ inch thick) and cook until the bottom is well browned and crisped, about 5 minutes. Flip and cook until the other side is well browned, about 5 minutes more. Sprinkle with salt. Serve immediately or keep warm in a low oven until ready to serve.

broccolini with kalamata dressing

SERVES 6 TO 8

⅓ cup pitted Kalamata olives
¼ cup lightly packed fresh
   flat-leaf parsley leaves, plus
   1 Tbs. roughly chopped
¼ cup mayonnaise

3 medium cloves garlic, peeled
Kosher salt and freshly ground
   black pepper
2 lb. broccolini, trimmed
   (4 bunches)

Put the olives, parsley leaves, mayonnaise, garlic, ½ tsp. salt, and ¼ tsp. pepper in a food processor and pulse into a coarse paste.

Bring a large pot of well-salted water to a boil. Working in 3 batches, boil the broccolini until tender, about 5 minutes per batch. Drain each batch well and keep warm in a large bowl covered with foil.

Dab the olive mixture over the broccolini and toss well to combine. Season to taste with salt and pepper. Transfer to a platter, sprinkle with the chopped parsley, and serve.

roasted rosemary butternut squash and shallots

SERVES 4

3 cups ¾-inch-diced peeled
  butternut squash (from
  about a 2-lb.squash)
4 medium shallots
2 Tbs. extra-virgin olive oil

1 tsp. chopped fresh rosemary
½ tsp. granulated sugar
Kosher salt and freshly ground
  black pepper

Position a rack in the center of the oven and heat the oven to 450°F.

Put the squash on a heavy-duty rimmed baking sheet. Peel and quarter the shallots and add them to the squash. Drizzle the oil over the vegetables; toss to coat. Sprinkle the rosemary, sugar, 1 tsp. salt, and ½ tsp. pepper over the squash; toss to coat.

Distribute the vegetables evenly on the baking sheet. Roast for 20 minutes. Stir, then continue roasting until the vegetables are tender and lightly browned, another 10 to 15 minutes. Before serving, taste and season with more salt if needed.

baby bok choy with warm miso ginger dressing

SERVES 4 TO 6

2½ Tbs. peanut oil
1½ Tbs. minced fresh ginger
½ Tbs. minced garlic
¼ cup mirin
½ Tbs. white miso
1 Tbs. fresh lime juice

1 Tbs. rice vinegar
¼ tsp. Sriracha
1 Tbs. Asian sesame oil
2 lb. baby bok choy, quartered
   or halved lengthwise

Heat ½ Tbs. of the peanut oil in a 12-inch skillet over medium-high heat until shimmering hot. Add the ginger and garlic, and cook, stirring, until beginning to brown, about 30 seconds. Whisk in the mirin, miso, lime juice, vinegar, and Sriracha, and cook until slightly thickened, about 1 minute. Stir in the sesame oil, transfer to a heatproof bowl, and keep warm.

Wipe out the skillet. Heat the remaining 2 Tbs. peanut oil over medium-high heat until shimmering hot. Add the bok choy, toss gently, and then cover and cook, turning occasionally, until crisp-tender and browned on some edges, 5 to 6 minutes.

Transfer to a platter, drizzle with the dressing, and serve.

citrusy beet, parsnip & radish slaw

SERVES 4

1 small navel orange
1 medium lemon
2 Tbs. finely chopped shallot
1 tsp. honey; more to taste
Fine sea salt and freshly ground
   black pepper
⅓ cup extra-virgin olive oil

3 medium beets, peeled, quartered,
   and cut into julienne
1 medium parsnip, peeled and
   cut into julienne
5 medium radishes, trimmed and
   cut into julienne
¼ cup ½-inch-long snipped chives

Finely grate the zest from the orange and the lemon. Squeeze enough juice from the lemon to measure 2 Tbs.

   In a large bowl, whisk the zests, lemon juice, shallot, honey, and 1 tsp. salt; let stand for about 10 minutes to mellow the shallots. Whisk in the oil in a slow stream and add a generous pinch of pepper. Add the beets, parsnip, radishes, and chives, and toss to combine. Season to taste with more salt, pepper, lemon juice, or honey. Serve right away for a refreshingly crunchy slaw or let sit for up to 2 hours for the beets to soften a bit.

stir-fried brussels sprouts with red pepper

SERVES 4

1 lb. small Brussels sprouts
  (3 cups)
2 Tbs. peanut oil
6 medium scallions, thinly sliced
  (white and green parts)
1 Tbs. minced fresh ginger
1 medium clove garlic, minced
¼ to ½ tsp. crushed red pepper
  flakes

1 medium red bell pepper,
  cored, seeded, and chopped
2 Tbs. lower-sodium soy sauce
2 Tbs. rice vinegar
Kosher salt

Trim any tough exterior leaves from the Brussels sprouts and halve each lengthwise. Slice each half lengthwise into thirds. Set aside.

Heat the oil in a large wok or 10-inch straight-sided skillet over medium-high heat. Add the scallions, ginger, garlic, and red pepper flakes and cook, stirring constantly, until fragrant, about 30 seconds. Add the Brussels sprouts and cook, stirring constantly, until they are bright green, about 4 minutes. Add the bell pepper, soy sauce, and vinegar. Cover the wok or skillet, reduce the heat to low, and simmer until the Brussels sprouts are crisp-tender, 6 to 8 minutes.

Uncover the wok or skillet, raise the heat to high, and bring the sauce to a full boil, stirring constantly, until reduced to a glaze, about 1 minute. Season to taste with salt and serve.

indian spiced cabbage

SERVES 4 TO 6

4 Tbs. unsalted butter
2 Tbs. canola oil
1 medium yellow onion, cut into
    medium dice
3 medium cloves garlic, mashed
    to a paste with a pinch of salt
2 tsp. finely grated fresh ginger
1½ tsp. garam masala; more for
    finishing

1 fresh hot red chile, such as
    Thai bird, Fresno, or serrano,
    seeded and minced
¼ tsp. ground turmeric
Kosher salt
1 large head green cabbage
    (about 3 lb.), outer leaves
    discarded, halved, cored, large
    ribs removed, and chopped into
    1-inch pieces (about 12 cups)

In a 12-inch nonstick skillet, melt the butter over medium heat until it begins to brown and smell nutty, about 4 minutes. Add the oil and heat for 1 minute. Add the onion and cook until softened and browned, about 6 minutes. Add the garlic, ginger, garam masala, chile, turmeric, and 1 tsp. salt. Cook, stirring constantly, until the chile softens, about 3 minutes.

Add the cabbage, stir well, cover, and cook, stirring occasionally, until crisp-tender, about 10 minutes. Season to taste with more salt and garam masala. Serve immediately.

tip

If you like things spicy, use a super-hot chile, like a Scotch bonnet.

carrot and sharp cheddar gratin

SERVES 8 TO 10

2 Tbs. unsalted butter; more at
   room temperature for the dish
1½ Tbs. extra-virgin olive oil
1 medium yellow onion, cut into
   ½-inch dice (about 1½ cups)
Kosher salt and freshly ground
   black pepper
1 cup plain panko
2 Tbs. chopped fresh flat-leaf
   parsley

2 tsp. chopped fresh thyme
1 cup heavy cream
1 Tbs. Dijon mustard
3 lb. large carrots (about 12),
   peeled, halved lengthwise,
   and cut crosswise into ½-inch-
   thick half-moons
4 oz. coarsely grated sharp
   Cheddar (1 cup)

Position a rack in the center of the oven and heat the oven to 350°F.
Butter a 9x13-inch (or similar) baking dish.

In a 12-inch skillet, heat the oil over medium-high heat. Add the
onion and ½ tsp. salt and cook, stirring occasionally with a wooden
spatula, until golden-brown, 7 to 10 minutes.

Meanwhile, melt the butter and pour into a medium bowl. Add the
panko, parsley, and thyme and toss well.

Whisk the heavy cream, mustard, 1½ tsp. salt, and ¼ tsp. pepper into
the onion, scraping up any browned bits, and then stir in the carrots.
Bring just to a boil, cover, lower the heat to medium low, and simmer
until the carrots are crisp-tender, 10 to 12 minutes.

Spread the carrot mixture evenly in the prepared dish. Scatter the Cheddar over the carrots, top with the panko mixture, and bake until the carrots are tender when pierced with a fork and the crumbs are golden-brown, 30 to 40 minutes. Let rest for 15 minutes before serving.

tip

Parcooking the carrots in the cream adds an extra infusion of flavor.

cauliflower with brown butter, pears, sage & hazelnuts

SERVES 8 TO 10

6 Tbs. unsalted butter

1 medium head cauliflower, cut into small florets about ¾ inch wide

½ cup toasted, skinned, chopped hazelnuts

8 fresh sage leaves, thinly sliced crosswise

Kosher salt and freshly ground black pepper

2 large ripe pears, cored and thinly sliced

2 Tbs. chopped fresh flat-leaf parsley

Melt the butter in a 12-inch skillet over medium-high heat until light brown and bubbly. Add the cauliflower, hazelnuts, and sage. Cook for 2 minutes, stirring occasionally. Season with 1 tsp. salt and ½ tsp. pepper and continue cooking, stirring occasionally, until the cauliflower is browned and crisp-tender, another 6 to 7 minutes.

Remove the pan from the heat. Add the pear slices and parsley. Gently toss to combine and warm the pears. Season to taste with more salt. Serve hot or at room temperature.

sautéed escarole with raisins, pine nuts & capers

SERVES 4

Kosher salt

2 lb. escarole (about 2 heads), trimmed, rinsed, and cut into roughly 2-inch pieces

2 Tbs. extra-virgin olive oil

3 large cloves garlic, smashed and peeled

2 Tbs. pine nuts

2 Tbs. raisins

1 Tbs. capers, rinsed

Pinch of crushed red pepper flakes

1 tsp. fresh lemon juice

Bring a large pot of well-salted water to a boil over high heat. Add the escarole and cook until the stem pieces start to soften, about 2 minutes (the water needn't return to a boil). Drain, run under cold water to cool, and drain again.

In a 12-inch skillet, heat the olive oil and garlic over medium heat, stirring occasionally, until the garlic browns lightly, 2 to 3 minutes. Remove the garlic with tongs and discard. Add the pine nuts, raisins, capers, and pepper flakes and cook, stirring, until the pine nuts are golden and the raisins puff, about 1 minute. Add the escarole, increase the heat to medium high, and cook, tossing often, until heated through and tender, 3 to 4 minutes. Sprinkle with the lemon juice and season to taste with salt.

rainbow chard with lemon, fennel & parmigiano

SERVES 8

- 4 large bunches rainbow or Swiss chard (about 3½ lb.)
- Kosher salt and freshly ground black pepper
- 2 cups thinly sliced fennel bulb, plus ½ cup chopped fronds (fronds optional)
- 2 medium lemons
- 6 Tbs. extra-virgin olive oil
- 6 medium cloves garlic, peeled and thinly sliced
- ½ cup freshly shaved Parmigiano-Reggiano (shave with a vegetable peeler)

Cut the chard stalks off just below each leaf and thinly slice the stalks. Chop the chard leaves into large pieces. Keep the stalks and leaves separate.

Bring a large, wide pot of salted water to a boil over high heat. Add the sliced fennel and chard stalks and cook for 3 minutes. Add the chard leaves and cook until tender, 3 to 5 minutes. Drain well in a colander. (The chard can be cooked to this point up to 3 hours ahead.) Rinse and dry the pot.

Finely grate the zest from the lemons and set aside. Cut the top and bottom ends off the lemons, then stand each on a cut end and slice

tip

Using the chard stems as well as the leaves gives this dish lots of extra flavor and texture.

off the peel to expose the flesh. (Remove all of the bitter white pith.) Cut the lemon segments from the membranes, letting them drop into a small bowl.

Heat the oil and garlic in the pot over medium heat. When the garlic begins to sizzle, add the fennel fronds (if using) and the lemon segments and cook, stirring often, for 1 minute. Add the chard leaves and stems and fennel and cook, stirring, until heated through. Stir in the lemon zest and season to taste with salt and pepper. Serve, sprinkled with the Parmigiano.

cranberry sauce with caramelized onions

YIELDS 2½ TO 3 CUPS

1 Tbs. vegetable or canola oil
1 large yellow onion, cut into medium dice
⅛ tsp. ground cloves
Kosher salt and freshly ground black pepper
One 12-oz. bag fresh or thawed frozen cranberries, rinsed and picked over (3½ cups)
1 cup granulated sugar

In a 10-inch straight-sided sauté pan or skillet, heat the oil over medium heat. Add the onion, cloves, a pinch of salt, and a grind or two of pepper. Reduce the heat to low, cover, and cook, stirring occasionally, until the onion is golden-brown and very soft, 20 to 25 minutes. Remove the lid, increase the heat to medium high, and cook the onion, stirring often, until deep caramel brown, an additional 2 to 3 minutes.

Add the cranberries, sugar, a pinch of salt, and ½ cup water and bring to a simmer over medium-high heat. Simmer for 1 minute, then cover, turn off the heat, and let cool to room temperature.

tip

The sauce may be prepared up to 3 days ahead and refrigerated. Return to room temperature before serving.

celery root-apple slaw with pecorino, parsley & and pine nuts

SERVES 6

1 medium celery root (about 1½ lb.), peeled, quartered, and cut into julienne
2 Granny Smith apples, quartered, cored, and cut into a julienne
1½ cups fresh flat-leaf parsley leaves, loosely packed
Flaky sea salt, such as Maldon®

4 oz. shaved Pecorino Toscano or manchego (about 1½ cups)
½ cup extra-virgin olive oil; more for drizzling
¼ cup pine nuts, lightly toasted
2 tsp. apple-cider vinegar; more to taste
Freshly ground black pepper

Put the celery root, apple, and parsley in a large bowl. Crumble 1 tsp. salt into the bowl and toss. Add most of the cheese, the oil, nuts, vinegar, and several grinds of pepper. Gently toss to combine well. Season to taste with salt and vinegar. Serve right away drizzled with more oil, sprinkled with additional pepper, and topped with the remaining cheese.

tip

Use nutty Pecorino Toscano, not romano; the latter is too salty here. If you can't find Pecorino Toscano, manchego makes a good substitute.

roasted baby red, white & purple potatoes with rosemary, fennel & garlic

SERVES 4 TO 6

1¾ lb. baby red, white, or purple
  potatoes, or a combination,
  scrubbed and halved
3 Tbs. extra-virgin olive oil
1 Tbs. chopped fresh rosemary
2 tsp. fennel seeds, crushed in
  a mortar or coarsely ground
  in a spice grinder

Pinch crushed red pepper flakes
Kosher salt and freshly ground
  black pepper
12 large cloves garlic, peeled
  and trimmed

Position a rack in the center of the oven and heat the oven to 375°F.

In a large bowl, toss the potatoes with the olive oil, rosemary, fennel seeds, red pepper flakes, ½ tsp. salt, and a few generous grinds of pepper. Arrange them cut side down in a well-spaced single layer on a rimmed baking sheet or in a shallow roasting pan, making sure to scrape out and include any herbs and oil stuck to the bowl. Roast for 20 minutes and then stir the potatoes with a spatula and scatter the garlic cloves over them.

Continue roasting, stirring every 15 minutes, until the potatoes are tender enough to pierce easily with a skewer and the skins are browned all over, crisp, and bit shriveled, about 45 minutes more. Serve immediately.

roasted root vegetables with meyer lemon

SERVES 4 TO 6

1 lb. carrots (about 5 medium), peeled, trimmed, cut crosswise into 3-inch lengths, then cut lengthwise into ½-inch-thick pieces

1 lb. parsnips (about 5 large), peeled, trimmed, cut crosswise into 3-inch lengths, then cut lengthwise into ½-inch-thick pieces, cores removed

1 lb. medium purple-top turnips (2 or 3), scrubbed, trimmed, and cut into ¾-inch wedges

1 Meyer lemon, top and bottom ends trimmed, quartered lengthwise and sliced crosswise ⅛ inch thick, and seeds removed

¼ cup extra-virgin olive oil

1 Tbs. finely chopped fresh rosemary

2 tsp. minced fresh garlic

½ tsp. ground cumin

Kosher salt and freshly ground black pepper

Position a rack in the center of the oven and heat the oven to 450°F. Line a large rimmed baking sheet with heavy-duty aluminum foil.

In a large bowl, combine the carrots, parsnips, turnips, lemon, oil, rosemary, garlic, cumin, 1 tsp. salt, and ½ tsp. pepper; toss to coat. Spread in an even layer on the baking sheet and roast, tossing once, until tender when pierced with a fork and golden-brown on the edges, 40 to 50 minutes.

Season to taste with salt and pepper and serve.

caramelized pineapple clafoutis

SERVES 6

½ large pineapple
   (14 to 16 oz., peeled)
4 Tbs. unsalted butter
¼ cup light brown sugar
3 large eggs
⅓ cup sugar

⅓ cup unbleached all-purpose flour
⅔ cup heavy or whipping cream
1 tsp. pure vanilla extract, or seeds
   from ½ split vanilla bean
1 Tbs. rum

Heat the oven to 350°F. Butter a 9-inch cake or pie pan.

Cut the half pineapple lengthwise into 4 wedges. Cut the core from each wedge, cut each wedge lengthwise again to make wedges about 1 inch wide, and then cut each of these crosswise into ½-inch slices.

Put the butter in a large frying pan over medium-high heat (ideally large enough to hold the pineapple in one layer). When it sizzles, add the pineapple. Give the pan a shake and then let the pineapple release its juices without stirring. Let the liquid bubble and evaporate, giving the pineapple only the occasional shake and stir. When most of the liquid has evaporated (after about 5 minutes), add the brown sugar and stir again. Let the sugar bubble for about 30 seconds and then remove the pan from the heat. With a slotted spoon, transfer the pineapple to the prepared cake pan; reserve the juices in the pan.

In a large bowl, whisk the eggs and sugar until lightly frothy and the sugar is dissolved. Sprinkle or sift in the flour and whisk until smooth. Add the cream, vanilla, and rum; whisk again. Finally, add the juices from the pineapple and give the mixture one last stir.

Pour the batter over the pineapple. Bake until evenly puffed and golden and a skewer comes out clean, about 50 minutes. Serve warm.

tip

Brown sugar adds a mellow sweetness to the pineapple, giving the clafoutis a complex blend of flavors.

free-form pear tarts with almond and cinnamon

YIELDS 4 TARTS

¼ cup granulated sugar
¼ tsp. ground cinnamon
1 sheet frozen puff pastry
(9¾-inch square), thawed
overnight in the refrigerator
Unbleached all-purpose flour,
for dusting

2 Tbs. almond paste (from a can
or tube)
4 tsp. sour cream
2 small firm-ripe pears (preferably
Bartlett), peeled, cored, and cut
into 12 wedges each

Position a rack in the center of the oven and heat the oven to 425°F.

Line a baking sheet with parchment. Combine the sugar and cinnamon in a small bowl. Unroll or unfold the puff pastry on a lightly floured surface. Pinch any creases together and then smooth them out with your fingertips. Cut the pastry sheet into 4 equal squares and transfer them to the lined baking sheet.

Roll 1½ tsp. of almond paste into a small ball, flatten it slightly with the palm of your hand, and put it in the center of one puff pastry square. Drop 1 tsp. of sour cream on top. Sprinkle about ½ Tbs. of the cinnamon sugar over the sour cream. Arrange four pear wedges in the center of the puff pastry, two leaning away from the center one way and two leaning the other way. Sprinkle with another ½ Tbs. of the cinnamon sugar. Repeat with the remaining 3 puff pastry squares and filling ingredients—you won't need all of the sliced pears.

Fold the corners of the puff pastry over the pears until the tips are just touching but not overlapping and press the dough against the pears. (The tarts won't look pretty now, but they'll be beautiful once they bake and puff up.) Bake until puffed and golden-brown on the edges, 22 to 27 minutes. Let cool. Any juices that leak onto the baking sheet will harden to a candy-like consistency, so break off and discard these bits before serving.

tip

Almond paste provides a subtle almond flavor that marries perfectly with the sweetness of the pears. You can find cans or tubes of almond paste in most grocery stores.

vanilla ice cream with kumquat–riesling sauce

YIELDS 3 CUPS

2½ cups Riesling
⅔ cup mild honey, such as clover
½ cup granulated sugar
Three ¼-inch-thick slices peeled fresh ginger
One 3-inch cinnamon stick

¼ vanilla bean, split lengthwise, seeds scraped out
12 oz. kumquats (2½ cups), sliced ⅛ inch thick and seeded
Vanilla ice cream, for serving

In a 4-quart saucepan, combine the Riesling, honey, sugar, ginger, cinnamon stick, vanilla bean and seeds, and ¼ cup water and bring to a boil over high heat. Add the kumquats and reduce the heat to medium low. Cook until the kumquats are tender and translucent and the liquid is syrupy, about 30 minutes.

Chill then serve over top of bowls of ice cream. The sauce will keep in the refrigerator for about 2 weeks.

tip

Look for kumquats that are bright orange to almost red, with firm, smooth skin and leaves attached (a sign of freshness). Traces of green may indicate an unripened fruit. Store kumquats at room temperature for up to 3 days or refrigerate for up to 2 weeks.

Recipe Index

COOK FRESH YEAR-ROUND

FALL

FROM

FINE COOKING

from the editors and contributors
of *fine cooking*

The Taunton Press

The Taunton Press
Inspiration for hands-on living®

The Taunton Press, Inc., 63 South Main Street,
PO Box 5506, Newtown, CT 06470-5506
e-mail: tp@taunton.com

Copy editor: Nina Rynd Whitnah
Indexer: Heidi Blough
Jacket/Cover design: Stacy Wakefield Forte
Interior design: Stacy Wakefield Forte

Recipes from: Tamar Adler, Pamela Anderson, Jennifer Armentrout, Robin Asbell,
Ben and Karen Barker, David Bonom, Arthur Potts Dawson, Melissa Denchak,
Tasha DeSerio, Maryellen Driscoll, Mary Ellen Evans, Kate Hays, Jeanne Kelley,
Alison Ehri Kreitler, Ris Lacoste, Ruth Lively, Lori Longbotham, Deborah Madison,
Ivy Manning, Susie Middleton, Dawn Yanagihara-Mitchell, Diane Morgan, Greg
Patent, Liz Pearson, Melissa Pellegrino, Laraine Perri, Elisabeth Prueitt, Julissa
Roberts, Tony Rosenfeld, Michael Ruhlman, Mark Scarbrough, Bruce Weinstein,
Jay Weinstein, Joanne Weir, Shelley Wiseman

The following name/brands appearing in Fall are a trademark: Jim Bean®,
Maker's Mark®, Pyrex®, Tabasco®, Wild Turkey®

Library of Congress Cataloging-in-Publication Data
CookFresh year-round : seasonal recipes from Fine cooking /author, editors of
Fine cooking.
    pages cm
  Includes index.
  ISBN 978-1-63186-014-0
1. Seasonal cooking. 2. Cookbooks. lcgft I. Taunton's fine cooking. II. Title: Cook
Fresh year-round.
 TX714.C65428 2015
 641.5'64--dc23
                        2014039388

Printed in China
10 9 8 7 6 5 4 3 2 1

fall

contents

cranberry-lime shrub sparkler

YIELDS ABOUT 1 QUART SHRUB, ENOUGH FOR 16 DRINKS

For the shrub
12 oz. (3 cups) cranberries, rinsed
    and picked over
1 cup granulated sugar
¾ cup Champagne or white-wine
    vinegar
1 strip lime zest (½ x 2 inches)

For each sparkler
1 cup cold seltzer, tonic water,
    or sparkling cider
1 fl. oz. vodka (optional)

In a 4-quart saucepan, combine the cranberries, sugar, vinegar, and lime zest with 3 cups of water and bring to a boil over medium-high heat. Reduce the heat to low, cover, and simmer until the cranberries are completely broken down, about 20 minutes. Let cool.

Purée with an immersion blender. Strain through a fine-mesh sieve set over a large bowl, pressing hard on the solids to extract as much liquid as possible.

Per drink, combine 3 to 4 Tbs. of the chilled shrub with 1 cup cold seltzer (and vodka, if you like).

tip

✴ The shrub—a sweetened fruit and vinegar syrup that's mainly used as a drink mixer—will keep, refrigerated in a jar, for up to 2 months.

kale chips with toasted lemon zest

SERVES 4 TO 6

9 to 11 oz. mature curly kale, trimmed
    and torn into bite-size pieces
3 Tbs. extra-virgin olive oil
2 tsp. apple-cider vinegar

2 Tbs. finely grated lemon zest
    (from about 2 large lemons)
Kosher salt

Position a rack in the center of the oven and heat the oven to 375°F.

Pile the kale on a large rimmed baking sheet. Toss with the olive oil and vinegar. Sprinkle the lemon zest over the kale and then season very lightly with salt.

Spread the kale evenly on the baking sheet and roast until it has begun to steam and dry out around the edges of the leaves, about 5 minutes. Using tongs, toss the kale, keeping it evenly distributed, and rotate the baking sheet to ensure even cooking. Continue to roast until the kale is dark green and shatteringly crisp, 7 to 10 minutes more. Some of the edges may begin to brown. Serve hot or at room temperature soon after roasting.

tip

Wash and dry the kale leaves well in advance of roasting to ensure that they are completely dry. Serve these snackable chips in a wide, shallow dish, or cool to room temperature in a single layer so they don't steam and become soggy. Either way, serve soon after roasting.

collard green crostini with blue cheese and grape-apple relish

YIELDS 24 CROSTINI

¾ cup apple cider

¼ cup golden raisins

½ Granny Smith apple, cored and cut into ¼-inch dice (1 scant cup)

½ cup red seedless grapes, quartered

1 Tbs. finely chopped fresh flat-leaf parsley

2 tsp. thinly sliced scallion

Kosher salt and freshly ground black pepper to taste

Twenty-four ½-inch-thick slices of crusty baguette

1 Tbs. extra-virgin olive oil; more for brushing

2 cups very thinly sliced trimmed collard greens (from 4 large leaves)

1 tsp. cider vinegar

5 oz. creamy blue cheese, such as Gorgonzola dolce or Roquefort

Position a rack in the upper third of the oven and heat the oven to 350°F.

Briskly simmer the cider in a small saucepan over medium heat until reduced to ½ cup, about 5 minutes. Add the raisins and set aside to cool.

Combine the apple, grapes, parsley, and scallion in a medium bowl. Add the cooled cider mixture and toss. Season to taste with salt and pepper.

Arrange the bread slices on a rimmed baking sheet and brush the tops with olive oil. Bake until crisp and pale golden, about 10 minutes.

In a medium bowl, toss the collard greens with the 1 Tbs. olive oil, the vinegar, and salt and pepper to taste.

Spread the cheese on the crostini. Top with the greens, pressing them gently so they'll stick to the cheese. Using a slotted spoon, top with the grape-apple relish. Serve immediately.

endive with apple, blue cheese & toasted hazelnuts

YIELDS ABOUT 20 HORS D'OEUVRES

½ large tart-sweet red apple, such as Braeburn or Gala, unpeeled and cut into ⅛-inch dice

⅔ cup crumbled blue cheese (about 1½ oz.)

⅔ cup finely chopped celery (1 large rib)

1½ Tbs. mayonnaise

1½ tsp. fresh lemon juice

Kosher salt

3 Belgian endives, leaves separated; smallest saved for another use

½ cup hazelnuts, toasted and coarsely chopped

In a medium bowl, combine the apple, blue cheese, celery, mayonnaise, and lemon juice. Stir gently to combine. Season to taste with salt.

To assemble, mound a small spoonful of the apple mixture onto each endive leaf. Sprinkle with the hazelnuts and serve.

tip

✧ The lemon juice in the apple filling slows down browning, so you can make the apple mixture hours ahead and then quickly assemble this nibble once guests have arrived.

roasted pepitas

1 cup pumpkin seeds, scooped from
   a pumpkin and cleaned of fibers
1 Tbs. grapeseed oil
Kosher salt

Position a rack in the center of the oven and heat the oven to 400°F. In a small bowl, combine the seeds and grapeseed oil. Spread the seeds on a large baking sheet and sprinkle lightly with salt. Roast until golden, 8 to 12 minutes. Let cool and serve warm or at room temperature. Roasted pumpkin seeds will keep for several days stored in an airtight container at room temperature.

quinoa salad with pears and dried cherries

SERVES 8 TO 10

2 cups white quinoa
Kosher salt and freshly ground
    black pepper
½ cup plus 1 Tbs. extra-virgin
    olive oil, more as needed
⅓ cup Champagne vinegar
2 tsp. honey

3 cups ½-inch diced pears
1 cup crumbled fresh goat cheese
¾ cup chopped toasted walnuts
½ cup chopped dried cherries
¼ cup chopped fresh tarragon

Rinse the quinoa under cold water and drain. Bring 7 cups of water to a boil in a 4-quart pot over high heat. Add ¾ tsp. salt. Add the quinoa, reduce the heat to a simmer, and cook uncovered, stirring occasionally and adding more boiling water as necessary to keep the quinoa covered, until tender, about 15 minutes. Drain and rinse the quinoa with cold water to stop the cooking.

Transfer the quinoa to a foil-lined rimmed baking sheet, drizzle with 1 Tbs. of the olive oil, and toss lightly to coat. Spread the quinoa on the baking sheet and cool completely at room temperature or in the refrigerator.

Put the vinegar in a small bowl and gradually whisk in the remaining ½ cup of olive oil. Whisk in the honey. Taste and season with salt, pepper, and additional vinegar or olive oil as needed.

Put the cooked and cooled quinoa in a large serving bowl and toss to break up any clumps. Add the pears, goat cheese, walnuts, cherries, tarragon, and ½ cup vinaigrette and toss. Taste and season as needed with more vinaigrette, salt, and pepper, and serve.

tip

✣ Before cooking quinoa, rinse it well to rid it of its coating of saponin, a bitter, soapy-tasting natural substance that protects the plant from insects and birds. Most quinoa is processed to remove much of the saponin, so submersion and a good swishing in a bowl of cool water is all it takes to finish the process.

pecan, radicchio & asian pear salad

SERVES 4

¾ cup pecan halves, cut in thirds
   lengthwise
2 tsp. unsalted butter
Kosher salt
1½ Tbs. sherry vinegar
½ tsp. granulated sugar
Freshly ground black pepper
2 Tbs. roasted walnut oil
2 Tbs. extra-virgin olive oil

1 small head (4 oz.) radicchio, cored,
   leaves separated and torn into 3 or
   4 pieces (4 lightly packed cups)
3 oz. frisée, trimmed and torn into
   bite-size pieces (4 lightly packed
   cups)
1 medium (9 oz.) Asian pear,
   quartered lengthwise, cored, and
   thinly sliced crosswise (1 cup)

Position a rack in the center of the oven and heat the oven to 350°F.

Put the pecans on a small rimmed baking sheet and toast until fragrant and pale golden on the cut sides, 6 to 8 minutes. Add the butter and ½ tsp. salt and toss with two heatproof spatulas until the butter is melted and absorbed by the nuts. Set the nuts aside (they can be added to the salad warm or at room temperature).

In a small bowl, whisk together the vinegar, sugar, and ¼ tsp. each salt and pepper. Slowly whisk in the oils until well combined.

Combine the radicchio, frisée, and pear in a large salad bowl and toss with just enough vinaigrette to coat. Add the nuts, toss, and serve.

kale salad with cranberry vinaigrette

SERVES 4 TO 6

½ cup fresh cranberries, rinsed and picked over
1 medium navel orange
2 Tbs. red-wine vinegar
1 Tbs. cranberry juice
1 Tbs. honey
4 Tbs. extra-virgin olive oil

2 tsp. finely grated peeled fresh ginger
Kosher salt and freshly ground black pepper
5 oz. mature curly kale leaves, trimmed and coarsely chopped, or baby kale (5 cups)

Pulse the cranberries in a mini or regular food processor until finely chopped, about fifteen 1-second pulses. Set aside.

Using a sharp paring knife, cut off the ends of the orange to expose a circle of flesh. Stand the orange on an end and pare off the peel and pith in strips. Quarter the orange lengthwise; slice each quarter crosswise into ¼-inch-thick pieces.

Whisk together the vinegar, cranberry juice, and honey in a large bowl. Slowly whisk in the olive oil. Whisk in the ginger and chopped cranberries and season to taste with salt and pepper.

Toss the kale and the orange pieces in the dressing. Season to taste with salt and pepper. Let sit for 15 minutes to 1 hour before serving.

fuyu persimmon and fennel salad with hazelnuts

SERVES 6

6 Tbs. fresh orange juice
2 Tbs. white-wine vinegar
2 Tbs. minced shallot
2 tsp. finely grated orange zest
Kosher salt and freshly ground black pepper
½ cup extra-virgin olive oil
4 medium ripe Fuyu persimmons, peeled, quartered, cored, and thinly sliced
2 medium bulbs fennel, trimmed, cored, and very thinly sliced or shaved
⅓ cup lightly packed fresh flat-leaf parsley leaves, coarsely torn if large
½ cup toasted, peeled hazelnuts, chopped
½ cup shaved Parmigiano-Reggiano

Put the orange juice, vinegar, shallot, zest, and ¼ tsp. salt in a small bowl and let sit for 15 to 30 minutes to soften the shallot and meld the flavors. Gradually whisk in the oil.

In a large bowl, toss the persimmons, fennel, and parsley with enough of the vinaigrette to coat (you may not need all of it). Season to taste with salt and pepper. Divide among six salad plates and sprinkle with the hazelnuts and Parmigiano.

tip

Fuyu persimmons have a subtle, crisp flavor reminiscent of apricots. Remove the core before eating and cooking. The skin is edible, though you may want to peel it, because it can be a little waxy.

baby greens with chicken, dried cherries, pears & pecans

SERVES 4 TO 6 AS A MAIN COURSE

1 medium clove garlic
Kosher salt and freshly ground black pepper
3 Tbs. extra-virgin olive oil
1 Tbs. red-wine vinegar
1 tsp. fresh thyme leaves
1 medium firm-ripe pear, peeled, cored, and cut into ½-inch dice

⅓ cup dried tart cherries
8 oz. packaged herb salad or mixed baby greens (8 loosely packed cups)
2 cups shredded cooked chicken
½ cup pecans, toasted

Chop the garlic, sprinkle with ½ tsp. salt, and mash to a paste with the flat side of a chef's knife. Put the paste in a large serving bowl and whisk in the olive oil, vinegar, thyme, and ¼ tsp. pepper. Gently stir in the pear and cherries. Add the greens, chicken, and pecans and toss to coat. Season to taste with more salt and pepper and serve immediately.

tip

Rotisserie chicken is a time saver in this salad. Feel free to substitute your favorite lettuces for the herb salad or mixed greens.

mediterranean kale and white bean soup with sausage

YIELDS ABOUT 10 CUPS; SERVES 6 TO 8

½ lb. sweet Italian sausage (about 3 links)

2 Tbs. olive oil

½ small yellow onion, cut into small dice

1 medium carrot, cut into small dice

1 rib celery, cut into small dice

5 large cloves garlic, minced (about 2 Tbs.)

⅛ tsp. crushed red pepper flakes

Kosher salt and freshly ground black pepper

6 cups lower-salt chicken broth

One 1-lb. 3-oz. can cannellini or white kidney beans, rinsed and drained, or 2 cups cooked dried beans

1 lb. kale, rinsed, stems removed, and leaves torn into bite-size pieces (8 cups firmly packed)

1 Tbs. fresh lemon juice

½ tsp. finely grated lemon zest (optional)

Remove the sausage from its casing and tear it by hand into bite-size pieces. Heat 1 Tbs. of the olive oil in a 4- or 5-quart heavy pot or Dutch oven over medium heat. Add the sausage and cook, stirring occasionally, until lightly browned, about 5 minutes. With a slotted spoon, transfer the sausage to a plate, leaving any rendered fat in the pot.

Add the remaining 1 Tbs. olive oil to the pot, increase the heat to medium high, and add the onion. Cook, stirring frequently, until fragrant and beginning to soften, about 2 minutes. Add the carrot and celery and cook, stirring frequently, until they begin to soften and brown, about 2 minutes more. Be sure to scrape any brown bits from the bottom of the pan. Stir in the garlic, pepper flakes, ½ tsp. salt, and ¼ tsp. pepper and cook, stirring, until the garlic is fragrant, about 1 minute more. Add the chicken broth and bring to a boil over high heat.

When the broth reaches a boil, reduce the heat to medium, add the sausage along with any collected juices, and half of the beans. Mash the remaining beans with a fork or wooden spoon and add them to the pot, stirring to distribute. Stir in the kale, adjust the heat as necessary to maintain a gentle simmer, and simmer until the kale is tender, 15 to 20 minutes. Stir in the lemon juice and lemon zest (if using) and season to taste with salt and pepper.

tip

You can serve the soup as soon as the kale is tender, but letting it sit for an hour and then reheating gently makes it even better (wait to add the lemon until just before serving).

curried carrot soup with cilantro

SERVES 4 TO 6

2 Tbs. vegetable oil
1½ lb. carrots, cut into 1-inch
   chunks (about 4 cups)
1 large yellow onion, cut into
   1-inch chunks
3 large cloves garlic, thinly sliced
1 tsp. curry powder
3 cups lower-salt chicken broth

Kosher salt and freshly ground
   black pepper
1½ cups carrot juice; more as
   needed
¼ cup packed fresh cilantro leaves
Chopped peanuts, for garnish
   (optional)

Heat the oil in a 10- or 11-inch straight-sided sauté pan over medium-high heat until hot. Add the carrots and then the onion. Cook, stirring very little at first and more frequently toward the end, until the vegetables are golden brown, 6 to 8 minutes.

Add the garlic and curry powder and cook, stirring, for about 30 seconds. Add the broth and ½ tsp. salt and bring to a simmer over medium-high heat. Reduce the heat to low, cover, and simmer until the vegetables are very tender, 10 to 15 minutes. Add the carrot juice and cilantro.

Purée the soup in a blender, working in two batches and making sure to vent the blender by removing the pop-up center or lifting one edge of the top (drape a towel over the top to keep the soup from leaking).

Return the soup to the pan, heat through, and season to taste with salt and pepper. If necessary, add more carrot juice to thin to your liking. Ladle into bowls and serve, sprinkled with the peanuts, if using.

tip

To keep tender herbs like cilantro at their freshest best, put them stems down in a few inches of water. Keep loosely tented with a plastic produce bag and store in the refrigerator.

eggplant ragoût with tomatoes, peppers & chickpeas

SERVES 4 TO 6

1½ lb. eggplant, preferably plump round fruits

2 Tbs. olive oil; more for brushing the eggplant

1 large red onion, cut into ½-inch dice

1 large red or yellow bell pepper, cored, seeded, and cut into 1-inch pieces

2 plump cloves garlic, thinly sliced

2 tsp. paprika

1 tsp. ground cumin

Generous pinch cayenne

2 Tbs. tomato paste

1¼ cups water

5 plum tomatoes, peeled, quartered lengthwise, and seeded

One 15-oz. can chickpeas (preferably organic), rinsed and drained

1 tsp. kosher salt; more to taste

¼ cup coarsely chopped fresh flat-leaf parsley

Freshly ground black pepper

Heat the broiler. Cut the eggplant crosswise into ¾-inch rounds and brush both sides with olive oil. Broil until light gold on each side, about 2 minutes per side. Let cool and cut into 1-inch pieces.

In a medium Dutch oven, heat the 2 Tbs. olive oil over medium-high heat. Add the onion and bell pepper; sauté until the onion is lightly browned, 12 to 15 minutes. During the last few minutes of browning, add the garlic, paprika, cumin, and cayenne. Stir in the tomato paste and cook, stirring, for 1 minute. Stir in ¼ cup of the water and boil, using a wooden spoon to scrape up the juices from the bottom of the pan. Add the tomatoes, eggplant, chickpeas, remaining 1 cup water, and salt. Bring to a boil and then simmer, covered, until the vegetables are quite tender, about 25 minutes, stirring once or twice. Stir in the parsley and black pepper to taste, and serve.

tip

✧ Buy eggplant with smooth, shiny skin that's unwrinkled. The fruit should feel firm and spring back slightly when you touch it. Soft fruit with a dull peel is likely too mature and will taste bitter.

stir-fried noodles with beef and vegetables

SERVES 4

3 oz. bean threads (cellophane noodles) or thin rice noodles
¼ cup canola or peanut oil
3 Tbs. soy sauce
1½ Tbs. Asian sesame oil
1½ Tbs. rice vinegar
1 Tbs. light brown sugar
½ lb. flank steak
Kosher salt
1 small zucchini (about 6 oz.), halved and thinly sliced crosswise into half circles
1 cup matchstick-cut or grated carrot (1 large carrot)
1 small yellow onion, halved and thinly sliced crosswise into half circles
1 Tbs. toasted sesame seeds

Bring a 3-quart pot of water to a boil. Add the bean threads or rice noodles, remove from the heat, and let sit until just softened (they should still be plenty toothy), about 3 minutes. Drain in a colander and rinse well under cool, running water. Toss with 1 Tbs. of the canola or peanut oil, and spread out on a tray or large plate lined with paper towels.

In a small bowl, mix the soy sauce, sesame oil, rice vinegar, and brown sugar. Trim the beef of excess fat and slice thinly across the grain. Cut the slices into 2-inch pieces. Season the beef with salt.

tip

Traditionally, the noodles for this Korean favorite are made of sweet potato starch, though bean threads or thin rice noodles are also fine.

Heat 1½ Tbs. of the canola or peanut oil in a 12-inch nonstick skillet or large stir-fry pan over medium-high heat until shimmering hot. Add the beef and cook, stirring, until it loses most of its raw appearance, about 1 minute. Transfer to a large plate.

Add the remaining 1½ Tbs. oil and the vegetables to the pan. Cook, stirring, until they start to soften, about 2 minutes. Reduce the heat to medium and add the beef and the noodles. Stir the soy mixture and drizzle it over all. Cook, tossing until everything is evenly coated with the sauce and the vegetables are cooked through, about 3 minutes. Serve immediately, sprinkled with the sesame seeds.

seared duck breasts with pear-bourbon relish

SERVES 4

4 small or 2 large skin-on duck breasts (about 2 lb. total)
Kosher salt and freshly ground black pepper
1 Tbs. unsalted butter
¼ cup minced shallot
1 large firm-ripe pear, peeled and cut into ¼-inch dice
3 Tbs. bourbon
2 Tbs. light brown sugar
One 1-inch-wide strip lemon peel
2 tsp. fresh lemon juice
Pinch ground allspice
2 Tbs. dried sweetened cranberries
2 Tbs. coarsely chopped roasted unsalted pistachios

Position a rack in the center of the oven and heat the oven to 375°F.

Trim any excess skin off the edges of the duck breasts, score the skin in a ½-inch crosshatch pattern, and pat the breasts dry. Generously season both sides of each breast with salt and pepper.

Heat a heavy-duty ovenproof 12-inch skillet over medium-high heat until very hot, about 3 minutes. Put the duck skin side down in the hot skillet (cover with a splatter screen if you have one). Cook until the skin is deeply browned and crisp, 3 to 4 minutes. Transfer to a large plate and pour off the fat in the pan. Return the duck to the

tip

For cooking, a regular bourbon such as Jim Bean® or Wild Turkey® is fine. Save expensive single-barrel bourbons for sipping.

pan skin side up and roast until medium rare (125°F), 10 to 15 minutes. Transfer to a cutting board to rest.

Meanwhile, melt the butter in a 2-quart saucepan over medium heat. Add the shallot and cook, stirring frequently, until softened, 1 to 2 minutes. Stir in the pear, bourbon, brown sugar, lemon zest, lemon juice, allspice, and ¼ tsp. each salt and pepper. Cover and simmer until the pear is tender, about 3 minutes. Uncover and continue to cook, stirring occasionally, until just a little liquid remains, about 5 minutes more. Stir in the cranberries and remove from the heat.

Slice the duck breasts crosswise ¼ inch thick. Remove the lemon peel from the relish and stir in the pistachios. Serve the duck with the relish.

hoisin pork with napa cabbage

SERVES 4

1 lb. pork tenderloin, cut into ¼-inch-thick strips (about 3 inches long)

1 tsp. kosher salt; more to taste

3 Tbs. hoisin sauce

2 Tbs. soy sauce

1 Tbs. balsamic vinegar

3 Tbs. canola or peanut oil

2 tsp. minced garlic

6 cups napa cabbage, cut into 1½-inch pieces (about ¾ lb.)

1 red bell pepper, cored, thinly sliced, and cut into 2- to 3-inch lengths

¼ cup thinly sliced fresh chives

In a large bowl, season the pork with ½ tsp. of the salt. In a small bowl, mix the hoisin sauce, soy sauce, and vinegar.

Heat 2 Tbs. of the oil in a 12-inch nonstick skillet or large stir-fry pan over medium-high heat until shimmering hot. Add the pork and cook, stirring, until it browns and loses most of its raw appearance, about 2 minutes. Transfer to a plate.

Add the remaining 1 Tbs. oil to the skillet. Add the garlic, and once it begins to sizzle, add the cabbage and bell pepper. Sprinkle with the remaining ½ tsp. salt and cook, stirring, until the cabbage starts to wilt, about 2 minutes.

Add the hoisin mixture, pork, and half of the chives and cook, tossing, until heated through, about 1 minute. Let sit for 2 minutes off the heat (the cabbage will exude some liquid and form a rich broth), toss well again, and serve sprinkled with the remaining chives.

cavatappi with cilantro-pistachio pesto

SERVES 4 TO 6

Kosher salt and freshly ground
    black pepper
½ large head cauliflower, cut into
    small (½- to ¾-inch) florets
    (about 6 cups)
3 medium carrots, halved length-
    wise and then cut on the
    diagonal ½ inch thick

7 Tbs. extra-virgin olive oil
1 cup lightly packed fresh cilantro
    leaves
½ cup unsalted shelled pistachios
3 medium cloves garlic, peeled
1 Tbs. fresh lemon juice
¾ lb. dried cavatappi
2 large scallions, thinly sliced

Position a rack in the center of the oven and heat the oven to 475°F.
Bring a large pot of well-salted water to a boil over high heat.

Put the cauliflower and carrots on a heavy-duty rimmed baking
sheet. Drizzle with 2 Tbs. of the olive oil and ½ tsp. salt and toss to coat.
Roast for 10 minutes, stir, and continue roasting until tender and golden
in spots, about 10 minutes more.

Meanwhile, pulse the cilantro, pistachios, and garlic in a food
processor until finely chopped. With the machine running, add the
remaining 5 Tbs. oil and purée until the sauce is smooth. Add the lemon
juice and ¾ tsp. salt and pulse to mix.

Boil the pasta according to the package directions until al dente.
Drain well and return the pasta to the pot. Toss the warm pasta with the
roasted vegetables and pesto. Season to taste with salt and pepper and
transfer to a serving bowl. Sprinkle with the scallions and serve.

roast pork tenderloin with pears and cider

SERVES 4

1¼ lb. pork tenderloin, trimmed

1 tsp. olive oil

Kosher salt and freshly ground black pepper

2 Tbs. unsalted butter

2 firm-ripe Anjou pears, each peeled, cored, and cut into 8 wedges

½ cup finely chopped shallots

2 Tbs. sherry vinegar

⅔ cup pear cider or apple cider

3 Tbs. heavy cream

1½ tsp. Dijon mustard

2 tsp. fresh thyme, minced

Position a rack in the center of the oven and heat the oven to 500°F.

Pat the pork dry, rub it with the oil, and season generously with salt and pepper. Heat a heavy-duty 12-inch skillet over medium-high heat until very hot, and then sear the pork on all sides until golden-brown, about 6 minutes total. Transfer to a small rimmed baking sheet and roast until an instant-read thermometer inserted into the thickest part registers 140°F, 10 to 15 minutes. Transfer the pork to a cutting board, tent with foil, and let rest for 5 minutes.

Meanwhile, melt 1 Tbs. of the butter in the skillet over medium-high heat. Add the pears in a single layer and cook, flipping once, until just tender and lightly browned, about 3 minutes per side. Transfer to a plate and keep warm.

Add the remaining 1 Tbs. butter and the shallots to the skillet and cook, stirring, over medium heat until the shallots are just beginning to turn golden, 2 to 3 minutes. Add the vinegar and stir, scraping up any brown bits. Add the cider and cook until slightly reduced, 2 to 3 minutes. Whisk in the heavy cream, mustard, and thyme and cook until slightly thickened, about 3 minutes. Season to taste with salt and pepper.

Slice the pork and serve with the sauce and pears.

tip

The term "firm-ripe" means a fruit is just at the beginning of the ripening window. For pears, judge ripeness by gently pressing the neck of the fruit near the stem with your thumb; in this case, the fruit should yield only slightly.

spaghetti with brussels sprouts, pancetta & hazelnuts

SERVES 4

Kosher salt and freshly ground
   black pepper
2 tsp. olive oil
5 oz. pancetta, cut into ¼-inch dice
   (1 cup)
3 cloves garlic, smashed and peeled
¼ tsp. crushed red pepper flakes
10 oz. Brussels sprouts, thinly
   sliced; some whole leaves are
   fine (about 3 cups)

1 oz. finely grated Parmigiano-
   Reggiano (1 cup using a rasp
   grater)
1 Tbs. fresh lemon juice; more
   as needed
¾ lb. dried spaghetti
¼ cup coarsely chopped, toasted
   hazelnuts, preferably peeled

Bring a large pot of well-salted water to a boil.

Meanwhile, heat the oil in a 12-inch skillet over medium heat. Add the pancetta and cook, stirring occasionally, until crisp, about 5 minutes. Using a slotted spoon, transfer the pancetta to a paper-towel-lined plate. Add the garlic to the skillet and cook, swirling the pan, until fragrant, 30 seconds. Remove and discard the garlic. Add the red pepper flakes, Brussels sprouts, and ½ tsp. salt. Cook, tossing with tongs, until the sprouts are crisp-tender, 2 to 3 minutes. Stir in half of the Parmigiano and the lemon juice and remove from the heat.

Boil the pasta according to package directions until al dente. Reserve ½ cup of the cooking water, drain the pasta, and then add it to the skillet along with ¼ cup of the reserved water.

Cook over medium-high heat, tossing and adding more water as needed, until the Brussels sprouts are tender, about 1 minute. Stir in the pancetta and season generously with black pepper. Taste and season with additional salt and lemon juice, if you like. Serve topped with the hazelnuts and the remaining Parmigiano.

mustard greens with chorizo and white beans

SERVES 4

1 large clove garlic, minced (1½ tsp.)
¼ cup extra-virgin olive oil
5 oz. cured chorizo or linguiça, casings removed, cut into ⅓-inch dice (about 1 cup)
¾ lb. mustard greens, trimmed and coarsely chopped (about 12 cups)

1 ½ Tbs. sherry vinegar
One 14-oz. can Great Northern or cannellini beans, rinsed and drained
Kosher salt and freshly ground black pepper

Combine the garlic and 1 Tbs. of the oil in a small bowl. Set aside.

Heat 1 Tbs. of the oil in a 12-inch skillet over medium heat until shimmering hot. Add the chorizo and cook, stirring occasionally, until lightly browned, about 4 minutes. Transfer the chorizo to a paper-towel-lined plate and discard the hot fat.

Add the remaining 2 Tbs. oil to the skillet and increase the heat to medium high. As soon as the oil is shimmering hot, add the greens and stir frequently with tongs until wilted, 2 to 3 minutes. Push the greens to the outer edge of the pan, lower the heat to medium low, and pour the garlic-oil mixture in the center. Cook until fragrant, about 30 seconds, then pour the sherry vinegar on top and let sizzle for a few seconds. Add the beans and gently stir everything into the greens. Gently stir in the chorizo; remove from the heat. Season to taste with salt and pepper and serve.

broccoli and shiitake stir-fry with black bean sauce

SERVES 4

6 dried shiitake mushrooms, reconstituted in 1 cup boiling water for 20 minutes
¼ cup black bean garlic sauce
2 Tbs. Shaoxing wine (Chinese rice wine) or dry sherry
1 Tbs. cornstarch
2 tsp. Asian chile sauce or paste

1 Tbs. vegetable oil
4 tsp. minced fresh ginger
2 lb. broccoli, crowns cut into florets, stems peeled and thinly sliced
½ cup toasted cashews, coarsely chopped
Steamed rice, for serving

Drain the mushrooms, reserving ⅔ cup of the soaking liquid. Discard the stems and thinly slice the caps. In a small bowl, combine the reserved mushroom soaking liquid and the black bean sauce, wine, cornstarch, and chile sauce. Stir to dissolve the cornstarch and set aside.

Heat the vegetable oil in a 12-inch skillet over medium-high heat. Add the ginger and stir-fry until fragrant, 15 seconds. Add the broccoli and ¼ cup water, cover, and steam until the broccoli is just tender, 3 to 5 minutes. Stir in the black bean sauce mixture and the mushrooms and cook until the sauce is thick and bubbly, about 1 minute. Add the cashews and toss to combine. Serve with steamed rice.

leek and goat cheese frittata

SERVES 4

3 Tbs. unsalted butter
2 Tbs. olive oil
3 large leeks (white and light-green parts only), halved lengthwise, sliced on the diagonal ½ inch thick, and rinsed

Kosher salt and freshly ground black pepper
6 large eggs
1 tsp. chopped fresh thyme
3 oz. goat cheese, crumbled

Position a rack in the center of the oven and heat the oven to 350°F.

Heat 2 Tbs. of the butter and 1 Tbs. of the olive oil in a 10-inch, ovenproof nonstick skillet over medium-high heat. When the butter has melted, add the leeks and a generous pinch of salt and cook, stirring, until the leeks are tender and lightly browned, about 6 minutes. Transfer to a plate, spread in an even layer, and let cool briefly.

In a large bowl, whisk the eggs with 1 tsp. salt and several grinds of pepper. Add the leeks, thyme, and goat cheese and gently stir to combine.

Wipe the skillet clean and heat the remaining 1 Tbs. each butter and olive oil over medium-low heat. When the butter has melted, add the egg mixture and gently shake the pan to evenly distribute the leeks and cheese. Cook until the eggs begin to set around the edges, about 5 minutes. Gently shake the pan to be sure the frittata isn't sticking (if necessary, slide a spatula around the perimeter to release it).

Transfer the pan to the oven and continue to cook until the frittata is set in the center, about 5 minutes. Remove from the oven and let sit for about 2 minutes. Carefully slide the frittata onto a serving plate, cut into wedges, and serve warm or at room temperature.

tip

Leeks are notoriously dirty because they are grown with soil piled all around them. To clean leeks, slice lengthwise and hold under cold running water, using your fingers to gently swish the dirt away. When slicing into smaller pieces, rinse in a bowl of cold water, swishing the water around to remove the dirt.

pan-seared catfish with creamy greens

SERVES 2

Kosher salt and freshly ground black pepper
1¼ lb. curly kale or mustard greens (about 2 bunches)
3 Tbs. canola oil
1 medium shallot, thinly sliced (½ cup)
2 large cloves garlic, thinly sliced
½ cup crème fraîche or sour cream
1¼ tsp. sweet paprika
½ tsp. celery salt
⅛ tsp. cayenne
Two 6-oz. catfish fillets
1½ tsp. fresh lemon juice

Bring a large heavy-duty pot of well-salted water to a boil. Meanwhile, tear the kale leaves from their ribs. Discard the ribs and tear the leaves into bite-size pieces. Wash well. Cook the greens in the boiling water until tender, about 5 minutes. Drain in a large-mesh sieve, pressing firmly on the greens with the back of a large spoon to extract as much liquid as possible.

Using the same pot, heat 1 Tbs. of the oil over medium heat. Add the shallot and garlic and cook, stirring constantly with a wooden spoon, until tender but not browned, about 2 minutes. Return the greens to the pot, add the crème fraîche,

tip

Kale will keep in the refrigerator's crisper drawer in an unclosed plastic bag for 2 or 3 days. It will keep for a few days longer if wrapped in slightly damp paper towels before putting it in the plastic bag, but the longer you keep kale, the stronger its flavor will become.

and toss with tongs to combine. Season to taste with salt and pepper; remove from the heat, cover, and keep warm.

In a small bowl, combine the paprika, celery salt, cayenne, and ¼ tsp. each salt and pepper. In a heavy-duty 12-inch nonstick skillet, heat the remaining 2 Tbs. oil over medium-high heat. Brush the catfish with the lemon juice and sprinkle both sides evenly with the spice mixture. Put the fish in the pan, reduce the heat to medium, and cook until browned, 4 minutes. Carefully flip the fish with a spatula and cook until it flakes easily when tested with a fork, 3 to 4 minutes. Serve the fish over the greens.

pan-seared arctic char with olives and potatoes

SERVES 4

4 small red potatoes (about ¾ lb.),
  sliced ¼ inch thick
Kosher salt and freshly ground
  black pepper
4 skin-on arctic char fillets
  (about 5 oz. each), scaled
3 Tbs. olive oil

2 sprigs fresh rosemary,
  each about 3 inches long
½ cup pitted Kalamata olives
3 Tbs. roughly chopped fresh
  flat-leaf parsley
1 Tbs. balsamic vinegar
4 lemon wedges

In a medium saucepan over high heat, bring the potatoes to a boil in enough salted water to cover them by 1 inch. Reduce the heat to a brisk simmer and cook until tender, about 5 minutes. Drain. Set aside.

Pat the fish dry and season with ½ tsp. salt and ¼ tsp. pepper. Heat 1½ Tbs. of the olive oil in a 12-inch nonstick skillet over medium-high heat until shimmering hot. Arrange the fish skin side down in the pan so the fillets fit without touching. Cook undisturbed for 3 minutes. Flip the fillets and cook until the fish is cooked through, 2 to 3 minutes. With a slotted spatula, transfer the fish to a serving platter or plates.

Add the remaining 1½ Tbs. oil to the pan and heat until shimmering. Add the potatoes and rosemary and cook, flipping occasionally, until the potatoes are tender, 3 to 4 minutes. Add the olives, parsley, vinegar, and a pinch of salt and pepper; stir gently to heat. Arrange the potato mixture around the fish. Serve with the lemon wedges.

mushroom and spinach skillet strata

SERVES 4

4 oz. baguette (about a 9-inch piece), cut into ½-inch cubes
1 Tbs. unsalted butter
1 medium yellow onion, halved and thinly sliced
4 oz. cremini mushrooms, trimmed and coarsely chopped (1½ cups)
1 large clove garlic, minced

1 tsp. coarsely chopped fresh thyme
Kosher salt and freshly ground black pepper
4 oz. baby spinach (4 lightly packed cups)
4 large eggs
1 cup whole milk
¾ cup coarsely grated smoked Gouda

Position a rack in the center of the oven and heat the oven to 450°F.

Spread the bread cubes on a large rimmed baking sheet and toast in the heating oven until dry and pale golden, 3 to 5 minutes.

Melt the butter in a 10-inch ovenproof skillet with a lid over medium-high heat. Add the onion; cook, stirring occasionally, until tender but not browned, 3 minutes. Add the mushrooms, garlic, thyme, and ½ tsp. each salt and pepper. Cook, stirring occasionally, until the mushrooms are soft, 3 minutes. Add the spinach and cook until wilted, 1 to 2 minutes.

In a medium bowl, whisk the eggs, milk, ½ tsp. salt, and ¼ tsp. pepper. Add the cheese and bread, toss until combined, and transfer to the skillet. Evenly distribute the ingredients, then press down on the mixture to flatten it. Bake, covered, for 10 minutes. Uncover and continue to bake until set in the center, about 5 minutes more. Let cool briefly, then slice.

beef ragù over spaghetti squash with garlic bread

SERVES 4

¼ baguette, halved lengthwise
1½ Tbs. unsalted butter, melted
6 medium cloves garlic
Kosher salt and freshly ground
    black pepper
1 small (2½-lb.) spaghetti squash,
    halved lengthwise and seeded
1 Tbs. extra-virgin olive oil

1 lb. lean ground beef
1 small yellow onion, finely chopped
One 15-oz. can crushed tomatoes
¼ cup coarsely chopped fresh basil
¼ cup freshly grated Parmigiano-
    Reggiano

Heat the oven to 375°F. Arrange the bread cut side up on a foil-lined baking sheet. Brush it with the butter. Peel and chop the garlic. Divide the garlic in half and sprinkle one-half with a generous pinch of salt. Using the flat side of a chef's knife, mince and mash the garlic and salt together to form a smooth paste. Spread each piece of bread evenly with garlic paste and season with salt and pepper. Bake until light golden-brown and crisp, 12 to 14 minutes. Cut each piece in half to make 4 pieces total, and cover with foil to keep warm.

Meanwhile, arrange the spaghetti squash in a single layer in the bottom of a large, wide pot. (Don't worry if the squash halves don't lie completely flat in the pot.) Add ½ inch of water, cover the pot, and bring to a boil. Reduce to a simmer and cook until the squash is tender enough to shred when raked with a fork but still somewhat crisp,

15 to 20 minutes. Transfer the squash to a plate and set aside until cool enough to handle.

While the squash cooks, heat the oil in a 12-inch skillet over medium-high heat. Add the beef, the remaining chopped garlic, the onion, ½ tsp. salt, and ¼ tsp. pepper; cook, stirring to break up the meat, until just cooked through, 5 to 6 minutes. Drain and discard the fat if necessary. Add the tomatoes, basil, and ¼ cup water; stir well and bring to a boil. Reduce the heat to medium low and simmer for 10 minutes. Season to taste with salt and pepper.

With a fork, rake the squash flesh into strands, transfer to plates, and season to taste with salt. Ladle the beef ragù over the squash and garnish with the Parmigiano. Serve with the garlic bread.

chicken with apples and cider

SERVES 4 TO 6

½ cup plus 2 Tbs. hard apple cider
2 Tbs. Dijon mustard
1 Tbs. plus 1 tsp. chopped fresh tarragon
1 Tbs. chopped fresh flat-leaf parsley
1 Tbs. melted unsalted butter
Kosher salt and freshly ground black pepper
2 medium carrots, peeled and sliced on the diagonal ¼ inch thick
1 small fennel bulb, trimmed, quartered, and cut lengthwise through the core into ½-inch-thick wedges

1 large yellow onion, cut into medium dice
One 4-lb. chicken, cut into 8 serving pieces, trimmed of extra skin and fat, and patted dry
¼ cup crème fraîche
1 tsp. cornstarch
½ cup lower-salt chicken broth
1 tsp. cider vinegar
1 large Granny Smith apple (unpeeled), cored and cut into ½-inch pieces
1 large Braeburn apple (unpeeled), cored and cut into ½-inch pieces

Position a rack in the center of the oven and heat the oven to 400°F.

In a small bowl, mix 2 Tbs. of the cider, 1 Tbs. of the mustard, 1 Tbs. of the tarragon, 2 tsp. of the parsley, the butter, ½ tsp. salt, and ⅛ tsp. pepper.

Scatter the carrots, fennel, and onion over the bottom of a metal, glass, or ceramic baking dish that measures about 10x15x2 inches. Arrange the chicken pieces, skin side up, on top of the vegetables.

Brush the cider-mustard mixture over the chicken pieces and roast for 30 minutes.

Meanwhile, in a small bowl whisk the remaining ½ cup cider, 1 Tbs. mustard, the crème fraîche, and cornstarch. Whisk in the chicken broth, vinegar, and ½ tsp. salt.

Remove the pan from the oven and reduce the temperature to 375°F. Pour the crème fraîche mixture around the chicken and then scatter the apples around. Return the pan to the oven and roast until the vegetables and apples are tender and an instant-read thermometer registers 165°F in several pieces of chicken, 20 to 30 minutes.

Transfer the chicken to a warmed platter. Use a slotted spoon to arrange the vegetables and apples around the chicken. Sprinkle with a little salt and the remaining 1 tsp. tarragon and 1 tsp. parsley. Tilt the roasting pan so that the juices gather in one corner. With a large, shallow spoon, skim as much fat as possible from the pan sauce. Season the sauce to taste with salt and pepper and pour into a pitcher to pass at the table.

roasted beet sandwiches with herbed goat cheese

MAKES 6 SANDWICHES

8 medium beets, trimmed

1 Tbs. vegetable oil

¼ cup extra-virgin olive oil

3 small cloves garlic, minced

¼ cup thinly sliced chives

1½ Tbs. finely chopped fresh tarragon

Kosher salt and freshly ground black pepper

8 oz. fresh goat cheese, softened

¾ cup (one 7.5-oz. container) crème fraîche

1 tsp. chopped pink peppercorns

Six 4-inch pieces soft-crusted ciabatta bread

3 cups baby arugula

Position a rack in the center of the oven and heat the oven to 375°F. Arrange the beets in a baking dish that's just large enough to accommodate them, such as an 8-inch square glass baking dish. Drizzle the beets with the vegetable oil and turn to coat well. Cover the dish with foil. Roast the beets until tender when pierced with a paring knife, about 1 hour. Let cool.

Peel the beets and slice ¼ inch thick. Combine the beets, olive oil, garlic, 1 Tbs. of the chives, and ½ Tbs. of the tarragon in a medium bowl. Season to taste with salt and pepper.

In a medium bowl, combine the goat cheese, crème fraîche, peppercorns, and the remaining 3 Tbs. chives and 1 Tbs. tarragon. Season to taste with salt and pepper and refrigerate until ready to use.

Position a rack 6 inches from the broiler element and heat the broiler on high. Split the ciabatta pieces and lightly toast them cut sides up directly on the rack under the broiler.

Divide the beet mixture evenly over the bottom halves of the bread. Drop the cheese mixture by spoonfuls over the beets. Top the cheese with the arugula, dividing evenly. Place the top halves of the ciabatta over the arugula and press gently. Cut the sandwiches in half on the diagonal and serve.

browned-butter mashed potatoes

SERVES 4

1½ lb. red potatoes, cut into
   1-inch pieces
6 Tbs. unsalted butter
Kosher salt and freshly ground
   black pepper
Chopped fresh chives

Bring a pot of well-salted water to a boil. Add the potatoes and cook until tender, about 20 minutes.

Meanwhile, in a 10-inch skillet, heat the butter over medium heat until the milk solids are browned, about 5 minutes.

Reserve ½ cup of the potato cooking water, then drain the potatoes. Coarsely mash the potatoes in the skillet with the browned butter, moistening with a little cooking water if necessary. Stir in ¾ tsp. salt and ¼ tsp. pepper and serve garnished with chives.

roasted fennel with asiago and thyme

SERVES 4

2 large fennel bulbs (about
   2 lb. total)
2 Tbs. extra-virgin olive oil
Kosher salt and freshly ground
   black pepper

1 tsp. minced fresh thyme
⅓ cup packed grated Asiago

Position a rack in the top third of the oven, put a large heavy-duty rimmed baking sheet on the rack, and heat the oven to 500°F.

Trim the fennel, quarter each bulb vertically, and trim away most of the core, leaving just enough to hold the layers intact. Slice each quarter into 4 wedges.

In a medium bowl, toss the fennel with the olive oil, ½ tsp. salt, and ½ tsp. pepper. Remove the baking sheet from the oven and quickly spread the fennel on the sheet, with the largest pieces toward the edges of the pan. Roast until the fennel pieces are almost tender and the bottoms are lightly browned, about 18 minutes.

Flip the fennel, sprinkle with the thyme and then the Asiago, and continue roasting until the cheese is melted and golden, 3 to 5 minutes more. With a spatula, transfer the fennel and any lacy, golden cheese bits to a serving dish.

sour cream and leek mashed potatoes

SERVES 4

1½ lb. Yukon Gold potatoes, peeled and cut into 1-inch pieces
Kosher salt and freshly ground white or black pepper
2 Tbs. unsalted butter
2 medium leeks (white and light-green parts only), halved lengthwise, washed, and sliced crosswise into ¼-inch-wide pieces (about 1 cup)
½ cup sour cream, at room temperature
½ cup whole milk, heated; more as needed

Put the potatoes in a large saucepan and cover with cold water by at least 1 inch. Bring to a boil over high heat, add a generous ½ tsp. salt, and lower the heat to a steady simmer. Cover the pot partially and cook until the potatoes are just tender when pierced with a fork, 10 to 12 minutes.

Meanwhile, melt the butter in a 10-inch skillet over medium heat. Add the leeks and sauté, stirring often, until tender but not browned, about 6 minutes.

Drain the potatoes and return to the pan. Steam-dry over low heat, shaking the pan until the potatoes leave a light film on the bottom, about 3 minutes.

Mash the potatoes with a potato masher. Stir in the leeks, sour cream, and milk, adding more milk as needed to reach your desired consistency. Season to taste with salt and pepper. Serve.

acorn squash with rosemary and brown sugar

SERVES 4

One 2-lb. acorn squash (unpeeled), halved lengthwise, seeded, and cut into 8 wedges
1 Tbs. unsalted butter
1 Tbs. extra-virgin olive oil
½ cup dry white wine

3 Tbs. packed dark brown sugar
1 Tbs. chopped fresh rosemary
1 Tbs. fresh lemon juice
Kosher salt and freshly ground black pepper

Using a paring knife, score each wedge of squash lengthwise down the middle of the flesh. Heat the butter and oil in an 11- to 12-inch straight-sided sauté pan over medium-high heat. Arrange the squash in the pan in a single layer and cook, flipping occasionally, until deep golden-brown on all cut sides, about 10 minutes.

Carefully pour the wine into the pan, then quickly scatter the brown sugar, rosemary, lemon juice, ½ tsp. salt, and ⅛ tsp. pepper over the squash. Cover the pan, reduce the heat to low, and simmer until the squash is almost tender, about 10 minutes more.

Uncover the pan and increase the heat to medium. Flip the squash and cook until the liquid is thick and the squash is tender, about 5 minutes more. Transfer the squash to a platter, season with salt and pepper to taste, and drizzle any remaining liquid over the top, and serve.

carrot mash with orange and mint

SERVES 4 TO 6

2 lb. carrots, peeled and cut
    into 1-inch pieces
Kosher salt
2 Tbs. unsalted butter, cut
    into 2 pieces
2 Tbs. heavy cream

2 Tbs. extra-virgin olive oil
1½ Tbs. finely chopped fresh mint
½ tsp. finely grated orange zest;
    more as needed
Hot sauce, such as Tabasco®

Put the carrots in a 4-quart saucepan with enough cool water to cover by at least 1 inch. Add 1 tsp. salt and bring to a boil. Turn the heat down and cook at a gentle boil until the carrots can be easily pierced with a fork, about 25 minutes.

Drain well in a colander, letting the steam rise for a few minutes.

Meanwhile, heat the butter, cream, oil, mint, orange zest, ½ tsp. salt, and a dash of hot sauce in the saucepan over low heat until the butter is melted.

For a rustic texture, return the carrots to the pan and mash with a potato masher to the consistency you like. For a smooth texture purée the carrots in a food processor until smooth and then return them to the pan. Add the butter and cream mixture.

Season to taste with more orange zest, salt, or hot sauce before serving.

sweet-sour red cabbage

SERVES 6

1 Tbs. olive oil
6 oz. bacon (about 7 slices),
    preferably applewood smoked,
    thinly cut crosswise
1 large yellow onion (12 oz.), thinly
    sliced (to yield 2 cups)
1 small head red cabbage (about
    2 lb.), cored, cut into eighths,
    and thinly sliced crosswise
    (to yield about 8 cups)

1 cup dark brown sugar
¼ cup red-wine vinegar
Kosher salt and freshly ground
    black pepper

In a 5- or 6-qt. Dutch oven, heat the oil over high heat, add the bacon, and cook, stirring occasionally, until its fat is rendered and the bacon is crisp, 3 to 4 minutes. Add the onion and cook, stirring frequently, until soft and lightly colored, about 3 minutes. Add the cabbage and cook, stirring regularly, until just wilted, about 5 minutes. Add the brown sugar and vinegar, stir well, and let cook until the cabbage is wilted but still has a bit of crunch left to it, about 5 minutes. Season with ¾ tsp. salt and several grinds of pepper. Adjust the acidity or sweetness with a touch more vinegar or sugar if you like, and add more salt and pepper if needed.

carrots and parsnips with bacon and thyme

SERVES 4 TO 6

1 Tbs. fresh orange juice

2 tsp. red-wine vinegar

2 tsp. honey

2 Tbs. extra-virgin olive oil

¾ lb. carrots (about 4 medium), peeled and cut into pieces 2 to 2½ inches long and ½ inch wide

¾ lb. parsnips (about 4 medium), peeled, halved lengthwise, woody cores discarded, and cut into pieces 2½ to 3 inches long and ½ inch wide

2 large shallots, root ends trimmed, peeled, and cut into ¾-inch-wide wedges

5 sprigs fresh thyme plus ½ tsp. fresh thyme leaves

2 slices bacon, cut crosswise into 1-inch pieces

Kosher salt

Combine the orange juice, vinegar, and honey in a small bowl. Set aside.

In a 12-inch nonstick skillet, heat the oil over medium heat. Add the carrots, parsnips, shallots, thyme sprigs, bacon, and 1 tsp. salt; toss well to coat.

Cover the pan with the lid ajar by about 1 inch. Cook, stirring occasionally, until the shallots are limp and lightly browned and most of the carrots and parsnips have a little bit of brown on them, 8 to 12 minutes. As the mixture cooks, you should hear a gentle sizzle.

Uncover, turn the heat down to low, and cook, stirring occasionally and then gently pushing the vegetables back into a single layer so that most have direct contact with the pan, until the vegetables are tender and nicely browned, 12 to 16 minutes.

Remove the pan from the heat and discard the thyme sprigs. Stir in the orange-honey mixture and the thyme leaves, and season to taste with salt. Serve right away or let sit off the heat, partially covered, until ready to serve, and then reheat gently over medium-low heat.

tip

Cut the parsnips just a tad bigger than the carrots because they soften more quickly.

butternut squash with spinach, raisins & pine nuts

SERVES 4

2 Tbs. unsalted butter

1 small lemon, finely grated to yield ½ tsp. zest and squeezed to yield 2 tsp. juice

2 Tbs. extra-virgin olive oil

1¾ lb. butternut squash, peeled and cut into ¾-inch dice (about 4 cups)

Kosher salt

1 medium yellow onion, cut into ½-inch dice

¼ cup raisins

5 oz. mature spinach leaves, thick stems removed (about 5 packed cups)

1 oz. coarsely grated Parmigiano-Reggiano (about ¼ cup)

2 Tbs. toasted pine nuts

Melt the butter in a small skillet or saucepan over medium-low heat. Cook, swirling occasionally, until the milk solids turn light brown, about 5 minutes. Remove from the heat, add the lemon zest and juice, and swirl to combine.

Heat the oil in a 12-inch nonstick skillet over medium heat. Add the squash and ½ tsp. salt; toss well to coat.

Cover the pan with the lid ajar by about 1 inch. Turn the heat down to medium low and cook, gently stirring occasionally, until the squash begins to brown, 5 to 6 minutes. As the mixture cooks, you should hear a gentle sizzle.

Turn the heat down to low, add the onions and raisins, and cook, stirring occasionally and then gently pushing the vegetables back into a single layer so that most have direct contact with the pan, until the vegetables are tender and browned, 12 to 15 minutes more.

Add the spinach and lemon butter and toss gently until the spinach is wilted, about 1 minute. Remove the pan from the heat and stir in the cheese and pine nuts. Season to taste with salt. Serve right away or let sit off the heat, partially covered, until ready to serve, and then reheat gently over medium-low heat.

green beans with almonds and garlic

SERVES 6 TO 8

1½ lb. haricots verts (thin French green beans) or green beans, trimmed
2 Tbs. unsalted butter
2 Tbs. pure olive oil
½ cup slivered almonds

1 tsp. minced or pressed garlic (1 medium clove)
1 Tbs. fresh lemon juice (from 1 small lemon)
Kosher salt and freshly ground black pepper

Bring a 6- to 7-quart pot of water to a boil. Add the beans and cook until bright green and barely crisp-tender, about 2 minutes. Drain in a colander and rinse under cold running water until completely cool. Spread the beans on a clean kitchen towel and dry thoroughly.

In a 12-inch skillet, heat the butter and oil over medium-low heat until the butter melts and the foam subsides. Add the almonds and cook, stirring occasionally, until golden-brown all over, about 3 minutes.

Using a slotted spoon, transfer the almonds to a plate. Reduce the heat to low and add the garlic to the skillet. Cook, stirring constantly, until fragrant, about 30 seconds. Add the beans, increase the heat to medium, and cook, tossing occasionally, until crisp-tender and lightly browned in some places, 5 to 8 minutes.

Stir in the lemon juice and season to taste with salt and pepper. Transfer to a serving platter, sprinkle with the almonds, and serve.

moroccan vegetable ragoût

SERVES 4 TO 6

1 Tbs. extra-virgin olive oil
1 medium yellow onion, thinly
  sliced (about 1¼ cups)
One 3- to 4-inch cinnamon stick
1½ tsp. ground cumin
2 cups peeled and medium
  diced (½-inch) sweet potatoes
  (about ¾ lb.)
One 14- to 16-oz. can chickpeas,
  drained and rinsed

One 14½-oz. can diced tomatoes,
  with their juices
½ cup pitted green Greek or
  Italian olives
6 Tbs. fresh orange juice
1½ tsp. honey
2 cups lightly packed very
  coarsely chopped kale leaves
  (from about ½ lb. kale)
Kosher salt and freshly ground
  black pepper

Heat the olive oil in a 5- to 6-quart Dutch oven or other heavy pot over medium-high heat. Add the onion and cook, stirring frequently, until soft and lightly browned, about 5 minutes. Add the cinnamon stick and cumin and cook until very fragrant, about 1 minute. Add the sweet potatoes, chickpeas, tomatoes and their juices, olives, orange juice, honey, and 1 cup water; bring to a boil. Reduce the heat to medium low and simmer, covered, stirring occasionally, until the sweet potatoes are barely tender, about 15 minutes.

Stir in the kale. Cover and continue cooking until wilted and softened, about another 10 minutes. Season with salt and pepper to taste.

maple-roasted carrots

SERVES 6 TO 8

3 lb. baby carrots, preferably with green tops, peeled and trimmed, leaving ½ inch of tops attached
⅓ cup pure maple syrup
¼ cup pure olive oil
3 Tbs. good-quality bourbon, such as Maker's Mark® (optional)
⅛ tsp. cayenne
2 tsp. kosher salt

Position a rack in the upper third of the oven and heat the oven to 425°F.

Spread the carrots in a single layer on a large heavy-duty rimmed baking sheet. In a measuring cup, combine the maple syrup, oil, and bourbon (if using).

Drizzle the syrup mixture over the carrots and sprinkle with the cayenne and salt. Using your hands or tongs, toss the carrots to coat evenly.

Roast the carrots, undisturbed, for 15 minutes. Toss and continue to roast until tender when pierced with a fork, about 20 minutes. (You can roast the carrots up to 1 hour ahead; keep them at room temperature on the roasting pan. Reheat in the oven, or serve them at room temperature.) Transfer to a platter and serve.

tip

If you can't find baby carrots with the tops attached, use small carrots that are about ½ inch in diameter at the stem end.

sautéed beets and beet greens with red onions and garlic

SERVES 4

2 Tbs. extra-virgin olive oil
½ small red onion, thinly sliced
3 large cloves garlic, thinly sliced
4 medium beets (about 12 oz.
    without greens), trimmed,
    peeled, halved, and sliced into
    ¼-inch-thick half-moons

10 cups lightly packed
    stemmed beet greens
Sea salt and freshly ground
    black pepper
1 Tbs. red-wine vinegar

Heat 1 Tbs. of the olive oil in a 12-inch skillet over medium heat. Add the onion and cook, stirring often, until golden-brown, 4 to 6 minutes. Add the sliced garlic and continue to cook until the onion is very tender and browned, 1 to 2 minutes more.

Add the beets and stir until coated in the oil. Add ¼ cup water, cover, and cook until the beets are almost tender, 5 to 7 minutes. Scatter the greens over the beets and sprinkle with a couple pinches of salt. Cover and cook, stirring once or twice, until the beets and beet greens are tender, 5 to 7 minutes.

Remove from the heat and drizzle with the vinegar and the remaining 1 Tbs. olive oil. Season to taste with salt and pepper and serve.

brussels sprouts with pancetta and pearl onions

SERVES 6 TO 8

1¼ lb. fresh red or white pearl onions
(or thawed frozen pearl onions),
root ends trimmed

4 oz. thick-sliced pancetta,
cut into ¼x2-inch matchsticks

2½ lb. Brussels sprouts, trimmed
and halved lengthwise

4 Tbs. unsalted butter, cut into
4 slices

¼ cup dry white wine

1 tsp. sherry vinegar; more to taste

Kosher salt and freshly ground
black pepper

If using fresh pearl onions, bring a 3-quart pot of water to a boil over high heat. Add the onions and cook for 1 minute to loosen their skins; drain in a colander and rinse under cold running water until cool to the touch. Pinch each onion at its stem end to make it slip out of its skin. If it doesn't, use a paring knife to remove the skin. (You can prepare the onions to this point up to 1 day ahead; refrigerate in an airtight container.)

Cook the pancetta in a 12-inch skillet over medium heat, stirring constantly, until crisp, about 5 minutes. Using a slotted spoon, transfer the pancetta to a plate.

Add the Brussels sprouts to the skillet and cook, undisturbed, until lightly browned on one side, about 2 minutes. Flip and cook, undisturbed, until lightly browned on the second side, about 2 minutes more. Add the butter, wine, and onions. Cover and cook, stirring occasionally, until the sprouts and onions are tender when pierced with a fork and most of the liquid has evaporated, about 15 minutes.

Stir in the sherry vinegar and pancetta and season to taste with salt, pepper, and additional vinegar. Transfer to a platter and serve.

tip

Browning the sprouts first deepens their flavor, and adding wine to the skillet creates aromatic steam to cook them through (without making the dish taste boozy).

roasted beets with white balsamic and citrus dressing

SERVES 4

½ lb. beets (4 to 5 medium)
2 Tbs. extra-virgin olive oil
¼ tsp. kosher salt
¼ cup strained fresh orange juice
1 Tbs. white balsamic vinegar

1 tsp. fresh lemon juice
¼ tsp. sea salt; more to taste
Freshly ground black pepper
1 to 2 Tbs. chopped fresh chives
  (optional)

Position a rack in the center of the oven and heat the oven to 450°F. Trim, peel, and cut the beets into 1-inch wedges. Discard the greens or save for another use. Put the beets in a shallow 9x13-inch (or similar) baking dish, toss them with the olive oil and kosher salt until thoroughly coated, and then arrange them in a single layer. Roast the beets, stirring after 20 minutes, until tender when pierced with a fork or skewer and lightly browned on the edges, 30 to 40 minutes.

Meanwhile, whisk the orange juice, vinegar, lemon juice, sea salt, and pepper in a small bowl until the salt is dissolved.

Remove the beets from the oven and while they're still hot, drizzle the dressing over them, tossing to coat. Let the beets cool to room temperature to meld the flavors. Taste and add more sea salt, if necessary. Serve at room temperature or gently warmed, topped with the chives, if using.

honey-lemon-glazed cauliflower

SERVES 4

¼ cup extra-virgin olive oil
1 medium head cauliflower
   (1¼ lb.), cored and cut into
   1-inch florets (about 7 cups)
Kosher salt
1 medium red onion, finely diced
2 Tbs. honey

1 tsp. ground coriander
½ tsp. sweet smoked paprika
¼ tsp. crushed red pepper flakes
2 Tbs. fresh lemon juice
½ tsp. finely grated lemon zest
1 Tbs. chopped fresh cilantro

Heat 3 Tbs. of the oil in a heavy duty 12-inch skillet (preferably cast iron) over medium-high heat. Add the cauliflower and ½ tsp. salt and stir to coat. Cook, without stirring, until the cauliflower is browned on one side, about 4 minutes. Turn each piece over and cook, without stirring, until evenly browned on the second side, about 4 minutes more. Reduce the heat to medium and continue cooking, stirring often, until browned all over, about 4 minutes longer.

    Meanwhile, in a small bowl, stir 2 Tbs. water and the remaining 1 Tbs. oil with the onion, honey, coriander, paprika, and pepper flakes.

    Add the onion mixture to the skillet and cook, stirring occasionally, until the onion is softened, about 1 minute. Continue cooking, stirring constantly, until most of the liquid has evaporated and the cauliflower is glazed, about 4 minutes. Transfer to a serving bowl, stir in the lemon juice and zest, and garnish with the cilantro. Serve immediately.

collard greens with spiced pears and almonds

SERVES 4 TO 6

2 Tbs. unsalted butter
⅛ tsp. ground cinnamon
Pinch of cayenne
Pinch of ground cloves
1 Bosc pear, peeled, seeded, and cut lengthwise into 12 slices
Kosher salt and freshly ground black pepper

¼ cup thinly sliced shallots
2 Tbs. extra-virgin olive oil
1 lb. collard greens, trimmed and cut crosswise into ½-inch-wide strips (about 8 cups)
¼ cup slivered almonds, lightly toasted

Melt the butter in a small saucepan over low heat and stir in the cinnamon, cayenne, and cloves. In a medium bowl, gently toss the pear with the spiced butter mixture and ¼ tsp. kosher salt.

Arrange the pear slices in a single layer in a 12-inch skillet and sprinkle the shallots in the spaces between. Cook undisturbed over medium-low heat until the pears are golden on one side, 3 to 5 minutes. Gently turn over the pears and stir the shallots. Cook until golden-brown, 3 to 5 minutes. Gently transfer the pears to a plate, leaving the shallots in the pan. Add

tip

Briefly braising the greens helps tenderize them without robbing them of their color or turning them bitter.

⅓ cup water to the pan and stir, scraping the bottom of the pan. Transfer the shallots and any liquid to a small bowl or measuring cup. Wipe the skillet clean.

Heat the oil in the skillet over medium heat until shimmering hot. Add half of the greens, quickly stirring and turning with tongs. Once the greens have just begun to wilt, after about 30 seconds, add the remaining greens, turning and stirring briefly. Pour the shallots and liquid over the greens. Reduce the heat to a gentle simmer and cover with a tight-fitting lid. Braise until the collards are tender, about 5 minutes. Season to taste with salt and pepper and stir in the pears. Serve with the almonds scattered on top.

miso-honey-glazed turnips

SERVES 4

1 lb. trimmed and peeled turnips,
   cut into 1-inch wedges
   (about 2 ½ cups)
2 Tbs. unsalted butter

1 Tbs. white miso
1 Tbs. honey
Kosher salt

Put the turnips in an 8-inch-wide, 3- to 4-quart saucepan and arrange snugly. Add the butter, miso, honey, ½ tsp. salt, and enough water to just cover the turnips (about 2 cups). Bring to a boil over high heat.

Cook over high heat, shaking the pan occasionally, until most of the liquid has reduced to a syrupy glaze and the turnips are tender, 10 to 12 minutes. (If the glaze is done before the turnips, add about ½ cup water and continue to cook. If the turnips are done first, remove them and boil the liquid until syrupy.)

Lower the heat to medium and toss to coat the turnips with the glaze. Season to taste with salt and serve. (The glazed turnips can be kept warm, covered, for about 20 minutes.)

sautéed broccoli raab with garlic and lemon

SERVES 4

3 Tbs. extra-virgin olive oil
1 Tbs. minced garlic (2 to 3 large cloves)
Scant ¼ tsp. crushed red pepper flakes

Finely grated zest of half a lemon; plus fresh lemon juice to taste
Kosher salt and freshly ground black pepper
1 lb. broccoli raab, rinsed, trimmed, and blanched

Put the oil, garlic, and red pepper flakes in a 10- to 12-inch skillet over medium-low heat. Cook until the garlic is fragrant and starts to sizzle slightly, about 3 minutes. Reduce the heat to low if the garlic starts to brown. Stir in the lemon zest, ¼ tsp. salt, and a few grinds of pepper. Raise the heat to medium high and add the broccoli raab, turning to thoroughly coat in the oil and spices. Turn frequently until it is heated through, 1 to 2 minutes.

Turn off the heat, sprinkle lemon juice over the broccoli raab to taste, toss again, and season to taste with salt and pepper.

tip

✵ When buying broccoli raab, look for deep, bright-green color, crisp stems, and fresh leaves. Store it unwashed in the crisper drawer for up to a few days.

spaghetti squash with indian spices

SERVES 4 TO 6

1 small (3-lb.) spaghetti squash
1 Tbs. vegetable oil
1 tsp. brown mustard seeds
3 Tbs. unsalted butter
½ cup finely chopped
   yellow onion
2 tsp. minced fresh ginger
2 tsp. chopped garlic

1 tsp. cumin seeds
½ tsp. ground coriander
½ cup seeded and chopped
   tomato
1 small serrano chile, seeded
   and minced
Kosher salt
½ cup coarsely chopped cilantro

Position a rack in the center of the oven and heat the oven to 350°F. Halve the squash lengthwise and scoop out the seeds with a sturdy spoon. Set the squash halves cut side down on a heavy-duty rimmed baking sheet, and bake until strands of flesh separate easily when raked with a fork, 50 minutes to 1 hour. Taste a few strands—they should be tender. If not, continue to bake. Set the squash halves aside until cool enough to handle. Use a fork to rake the cooked squash flesh into strands.

    In a 10-inch skillet, heat the oil over medium-high heat until hot. Add the mustard seeds and cover. The seeds will start popping; cook until the popping subsides, about 1 minute. Uncover, reduce the heat to medium, and add the butter. As soon as it melts, add the onion, ginger, garlic, cumin seeds, and coriander and cook, stirring, until the onion is soft, about 3 minutes. Add the tomato, chile, and 1 tsp. salt and cook, stirring, until the tomato begins to soften and the chile is fragrant, about 2 minutes.

Increase the heat to medium high and add the squash to the skillet. Continue to cook, tossing with tongs, until heated through, 1 to 3 minutes. Toss in the cilantro, season to taste with more salt, and serve.

tip

Once cooked, spaghetti squash makes an unexpected ingredient in shredded vegetable salads or a great stand-in for spaghetti. Its mild flavor pairs well with just about any dressing or sauce. Store spaghetti squash for several weeks at room temperature.

spicy roasted sweet potatoes with orange and honey

SERVES 4

3 Tbs. unsalted butter; more for the pan
3 Tbs. honey
¼ cup orange juice
¼ tsp. cayenne

4 medium sweet potatoes (2 lb. total), peeled, halved crosswise, and quartered lengthwise
Salt and freshly ground black pepper

Heat the oven to 400°F. Lightly butter a large Pyrex® or ceramic baking dish. In a small saucepan, melt the butter. Whisk in the honey, orange juice, and cayenne. Put the sweet potatoes in the buttered baking dish, add the honey mixture, and toss the slices well to coat them thoroughly. Arrange the sweet potatoes in a single layer; sprinkle with salt and pepper. Roast until the potatoes are browned and tender and the juices are bubbly and thickened, 45 to 55 minutes. To ensure even roasting, stir and baste several times with the pan juices, doing so more frequently toward the end of roasting. Serve immediately.

grown-up applesauce

YIELDS ABOUT 1 QUART

8 Braeburn apples, peeled,
  cored, and cut into chunks
  (roughly about 1 inch each)
3 Tbs. unsalted butter
3 Tbs. water

½ vanilla bean, split lengthwise
3 to 4 Tbs. granulated sugar
1 to 2 Tbs. brandy

Put the apples, butter, and water in a heavy saucepan. Tuck the vanilla bean in among the apples, cover the pan, set it over medium heat, and simmer until the apples are completely tender and have cooked to a rough purée, stirring them gently from time to time, 20 to 25 minutes. Add the sugar, stir, and continue cooking uncovered for a few minutes to let the sugar dissolve. Taste the sauce for sweetness; it should be tart-sweet, but if you want it sweeter, add more sugar. Stir in the brandy and simmer for a few minutes more to cook off a little of the alcohol.

Remove from the heat and set aside to cool. Leave the vanilla bean in the applesauce to steep; remove it before serving. If not serving the same day, refrigerate for up to a week.

cranberry-orange relish with ginger

YIELDS 3 CUPS; SERVES 8

1 package (12 ounces) fresh cranberries, picked over and stemmed

1 small navel orange, including the peel, cut into eighths

A generous ⅓ cup roughly chopped crystallized ginger

1 tablespoon granulated sugar

¼ teaspoon kosher salt

In a food processor, combine the cranberries, orange, crystallized ginger, sugar, and salt. Process until coarsely ground, stopping once or twice to scrape down the sides of the bowl. Transfer to a serving bowl, cover, and refrigerate until ready to serve.

spiced pumpkin bread pudding

SERVES 12

Softened unsalted butter,
  for the dish
Two 15-oz. cans pure pumpkin purée
2 cups whole milk
2 cups heavy cream
2 cups packed dark brown sugar
8 large eggs
1 Tbs. pure vanilla extract
1 Tbs. ground cinnamon
1 tsp. ground ginger

1 tsp. freshly grated nutmeg
1 tsp. fine sea salt
½ tsp. ground cloves
1½ lb. challah, brioche, or other
  soft egg bread, cut into 1-inch
  cubes (about 16 cups)
Confectioners' sugar, for dusting
  (optional)
Unsweetened or lightly sweetened
  whipped cream, for serving

Position a rack in the center of the oven and heat the oven to 350°F.
Butter a 9x13-inch (or similar) baking dish.

Whisk the pumpkin, milk, cream, sugar, eggs, vanilla, cinnamon,
ginger, nutmeg, salt, and cloves in a large bowl until well blended. Fold
in the bread cubes and let sit at room temperature for 15 minutes so
the bread can absorb some of the custard. Re-toss and transfer the
mixture to the prepared dish. (If making ahead, cover and refrigerate
for up to 24 hours.)

Bake until a skewer inserted in the center comes out clean, 40 to
45 minutes. Transfer to a rack to cool slightly, at least 20 minutes.

Serve warm or at room temperature, dusted with confectioners'
sugar, if you like, and accompanied by the whipped cream.

pear fritters with lemon and ginger

YIELDS ABOUT 40 FRITTERS

2 small firm-ripe pears (preferably Bartlett), peeled, cored, and finely diced

1 Tbs. finely grated fresh ginger

½ tsp. finely grated lemon zest

1½ cups plus 1 Tbs. granulated sugar

2 tsp. plus ⅛ tsp. ground cinnamon

3 large egg whites

1 cup whole milk

1 tsp. pure vanilla extract

1½ cups unbleached all-purpose flour

2 to 2½ cups canola oil

In a small bowl, combine the pears, ginger, lemon zest, 1 Tbs. of the sugar, and ⅛ tsp. of the cinnamon. Macerate at room temperature for 15 minutes.

In a medium bowl, whisk the egg whites to soft peaks. In another medium bowl, whisk the milk, ½ cup of the sugar, and the vanilla until the sugar dissolves and the mixture is slightly frothy. Whisk in the flour just until combined—it shouldn't be completely smooth. With a rubber spatula, fold in the egg whites, and then fold in the pear mixture. In a small bowl, mix the remaining 1 cup sugar and 2 tsp. cinnamon.

Pour ½ inch of oil into a 10-inch cast-iron skillet with a candy thermometer clipped to the side. Heat over medium-high heat to 350°F. Using 2 tablespoons or a small ice cream scoop, carefully drop a ball of batter into the hot oil. Add 4 or 5 more to the oil, but don't crowd the pan. Fry until golden-brown, about 2 minutes. Using a slotted spoon, turn the fritters over and continue frying until golden-brown and cooked through, about 2 minutes more. Transfer to a paper-towel-lined plate and drain briefly. Toss in the cinnamon sugar to coat and transfer to a platter. Continue cooking the rest of the fritters in the same manner. Serve hot.

tip

To peel the ginger before grating, use the edge of a metal spoon to scrape off the skin. It takes a bit more effort than a paring knife or peeler, but it's less wasteful—and lets you maneuver around the knobs.

german pear pancake

SERVES 4 TO 6

1 large firm-ripe Bosc pear, peeled, cored, and cut into ⅛-inch-thick slices
1 large lemon, finely grated to yield ½ Tbs. zest, squeezed to yield 2 Tbs. juice
4 large eggs
¾ cup whole milk

¼ cup granulated sugar
1 tsp. pure vanilla extract
½ tsp. kosher salt
⅔ cup unbleached all-purpose flour
3 Tbs. unsalted butter, cut into 3 slices
3 to 4 Tbs. confectioners' sugar, for garnish

Position a rack in the center of the oven and heat the oven to 400°F.

In a medium bowl, toss the pears with the lemon juice and set aside.

In a large bowl, beat the eggs with an electric hand-held mixer on high speed until thick and frothy, about 3 minutes. Add the milk, granulated sugar, vanilla, salt, and lemon zest and mix on low speed until combined. Sift in the flour and mix on low speed until combined (don't worry if there are lumps).

Heat a 12-inch cast-iron skillet over medium heat until hot, about 2 minutes. Add the butter, and when it begins to foam, add the pear slices, quickly turning them to coat with the butter and arranging them in a single layer. Pour the batter evenly over the pears and transfer the skillet to the oven. Bake until the pancake is set in the middle, the sides have risen, and the bottom is nicely browned, about 20 minutes.

Sprinkle the pancake with the confectioners' sugar.

chocolate-pomegranate-ginger bark

SERVES 6

10 oz. bittersweet chocolate (60% cacao), broken into 1-inch pieces
1 cup fresh pomegranate seeds from 1 large pomegranate

1½ Tbs. minced candied ginger
¼ tsp. fine sea salt

Line a baking sheet with a silicone baking mat or waxed paper. Put the chocolate in a wide, shallow microwave-safe bowl and microwave on high until it just starts to melt, about 1 minute. Stir with a spatula until the chocolate is completely melted and smooth, heating in additional 15-second increments, if necessary.

Gently stir half of the pomegranate seeds, the ginger (break up any clumps with your fingers), and the salt into the chocolate. Scrape the chocolate mixture onto the baking sheet and spread it into an 8x10-inch rectangle. Sprinkle the remaining pomegranate seeds evenly over the top, pressing them into the chocolate.

Refrigerate until fully set, about 30 minutes. Break the bark into chunks with your hands (be careful not to crush the seeds), and serve. The bark will keep, refrigerated, for up to 5 days.

french apple turnovers

SERVES 4

1 Tbs. unsalted butter

1 large sweet apple, such as Gala or Honeycrisp, peeled, cored, and thinly sliced

1 Tbs. plus 1 tsp. granulated sugar

¼ tsp. ground cinnamon

Kosher salt

1 large egg

1 sheet frozen puff pastry (from a 17.3-oz. box), thawed overnight in the refrigerator and cut into four equal rectangles

Position a rack in the center of the oven and heat the oven to 425°F.

Melt the butter in a 12-inch skillet over medium heat. Add the apple slices and cook, stirring often, until softened, about 4 minutes.

Sprinkle 1 Tbs. of the sugar, the cinnamon, and ¼ tsp. salt over the apples; cook, stirring often, for 1 minute more. Remove from the heat.

In a small bowl, beat the egg with 2 Tbs. of water. Lightly brush the edges of each pastry rectangle with some of the egg wash. Spread the cooked apples and any juice over half of the long side of each rectangle, but not over the egg wash border. Fold the pastry half without apples over the side with apples, long side to long side. Press to seal the edges tightly and transfer to a large rimmed baking sheet.

Brush the tops with some of the remaining egg wash and sprinkle each with ¼ tsp. of the remaining sugar.

Bake until puffed and golden, about 16 minutes. Serve warm.

Recipe Index

Desserts